W0017678

ROYAL RECORDS

OF THE

DAUGHTER

OF THE

KING

The Paths We Take

Each day is a new opportunity to experience the power
of God in your life. Walk boldly into the future because
He holds the future and He is already there. He knows
what lies ahead and His thoughts for you are good.

LAUNA WALQUIST

My God My Everything
www.mygodmyeverything.org

Royal Records of The Daughter of The King
The Paths We Take

© 2021, Launa Walquist.

Print ISBN: 978-1-66781-9-549

CONTENTS

WALKING YOUR PATH

In our lives we will encounter many different types of paths. Some will be filled with anticipation of the destination, joy and excitement. Others will lead us to places of grief, disappointment and sorrow. How we navigate those paths and who we invite to join us along the way will have a tremendous impact on the whole experience and outcome.

The bible tells a story of two men who were walking a path of loss and discouragement. Their pain was evident and they felt hopeless. But their story and path didn't end there. Along the way they were joined by another traveler who listened as they described the cause of their pain and responded by sharing the truth of their situation.

As he spoke and explained scripture to them, their minds were opened up to understand and their hearts burned within them. They invited him to stay with them and break bread together. When they broke bread their eyes were opened and they recognized that the fellow traveler was none other than Jesus himself, the Risen Lord! Immediately they returned to Jerusalem to share the Good News with others.

Every day we have the privilege of inviting Jesus to join us on our paths of life. He is always willing to listen to us and will respond with the truth of His Word. He provides us with our Daily Bread which means that everything we need can be found in Him.

The paths we walk will supply opportunities for His Holy Spirit to work in us to produce the Fruit of the Spirit that will make us more like Jesus and be a witness to others of His presence in our lives.

I pray that this book will help you document your journey with Jesus and to recognize His provision, grace and purpose in your daily life. I hope your heart burns within you as you experience His presence and that you find a passion for His Word as He opens your mind to understand scripture. Remember who you are and who you represent. You are a Daughter of The King! May God bless you on your journey.

YOUR ROYAL LINEAGE

Fear not! I have redeemed you and called you by name. You are mine.

Isaiah 43:1

Did you know that you are Royalty? Not only are you Royalty but you have been placed in your exact circumstances for such a time as this. God determined the times set for us and the exact places that we should live. (Acts 17:26) Your current location is part of God's plan for your destiny.

Fill in the blanks with your name and embrace your Royal Identity.

John 1: 12 _____ **is God's daughter.**

"But _____ received Him, and to _____ He gave the right to become God's daughter, because _____ believes in His name."

John 15:5 _____ **is part of the true vine, and a channel of Christ's life.**

"I am the vine. _____ is the branch. If _____ remains in Me, and I in her, she will bear much fruit, for apart from Me, _____ can do nothing."

Romans 8:17 _____ **is a joint heir with Christ, she shares Christ's inheritance with Him.**

"And if a daughter, then an heir; an heir of God and a joint-heir with Christ; if indeed _____ suffers with Him, that _____ may also be glorified with Him.

Ephesians 1: 5-6 _____ **has been adopted by God as His daughter.**

"Having predestined _____ for adoption as a daughter through Jesus Christ to Himself, according to the good pleasure of His desire, to the praise of the glory of His grace, by which He freely bestowed favor on _____ in the Beloved."

Ephesians 1:1 _____ has an inheritance in Christ.

"In Him also _____ was assigned an inheritance, having been predestined according to the purpose of Him who works all things after the counsel of His will."

Ephesians 2: 5-6 _____ has been made alive with Christ and she is seated with Christ in heavenly places.

"Even when _____ was dead in her trespasses God made her alive together with Christ (by grace _____ has been saved), and raised _____ up with Him and made _____ to sit with Him in the heavenly places in Christ Jesus."

Ephesians 2:10 _____ is God's workmanship, His handiwork

"For _____ is His workmanship, created in Christ Jesus for good works, which God prepared before that _____ should walk in them."

Colossians 1:27 Christ Himself is in _____.

"To whom God was pleased to make known what are the riches of the glory of this mystery among the Gentiles, which is Christ in _____, the hope of glory."

Colossians 3:3 _____'s life is hidden with Christ in God.

"For _____ died, and her life is hidden with Christ in God."

In Christ you have life and purpose. Because of His free gifts of mercy and grace you can choose to accept the position and destiny that He planned for you before the creation of the world. That position is Daughter of the King. Royalty.

He has told you through His word that all of your days were written in His book before one of them came into being and that you are His masterpiece that is beautifully and wonderfully made.

You are chosen, redeemed and called to be an Ambassador of the King; His witness to those in your sphere of influence. In that calling God has equipped you for any and every situation that will arise on your life's journey. He invites you to walk joyfully with Him along the pathway of your life on this adventure together and gives you the promise that you are never alone. He will always be with you

He did this so that you would have confidence in His promises and choose to set out on the greatest adventure you could ever imagine; discovering God through a personal relationship with Him.

Each day is a new opportunity to experience His presence in your life. He knows all, sees all and is over all; a constant companion, who better to be on a journey with than the Creator of the Universe. In this life's journey you will have many opportunities to discover the endless characteristics of God.

Royal Records will help you document your journey and see how God is leading you, positioning you and training you to be all that He created you to be. Share your praises and prayer requests as well as your moments of joy, sorrows and thankfulness for both. Be Intentional about writing down the teaching moments from His word and life events as well as Divine Encounters that He has orchestrated along the way.

Live a life of joyful expectation for what God will do next! Remember, You are a daughter of the King of Kings. Your life explodes with significance and He is waiting to show you your true value and worth to Him. His love for you is unconditional and unending and He desires to be included in every moment of your life....so invite Him on this journey with you. The relationship that will result in the greatest treasure you will ever know.

MAKE A DECISION

Now that you have a little better understanding of what it means to be Royalty in God's eyes you have a decision to make. Do you accept the title along with the responsibilities and blessings that come with being a Daughter of the King?

The bible teaches us to weigh the costs involved before making such an eternal decision. The pathway of following Jesus isn't always easy. There will be trials, temptations and tests but there will also be moments of victory, exceeding joy and peace that surpasses understanding.

God has promised to never leave you nor forsake you and as a believer He has provided His Holy Spirit to live within you to guide and direct you. The beginning of your journey starts the moment you make your decision. He has also revealed the final destination which is eternity with Him. The journey in between is the adventure that awaits you as you discover who Christ is in your personal relationship with Him.

To begin, simply pray this prayer with a sincere heart and step out into the most incredible experience of your life.

Dear Lord Jesus, I know that I am a sinner, and I ask for Your for-giveness. I believe You died for my sins and rose from the dead. I turn from my sins and invite You to come into my heart and life. I want to trust and follow You as my Lord and Savior. In your name, amen.

WELCOME TO THE ROYAL FAMILY!

As a member of the Royal Family you are an Ambassador of Christ and have been chosen to represent Him. Believers are citizens of Heaven and are Christ's representatives here on earth. You are called to follow His example of loving God and loving people.

Throughout your journey here on earth you will always have complete access to God. You can approach His throne with confidence knowing that He is a good Father, He is Holy, He is sovereign and His love is unconditional. Visit the throne room often. He desires to hear from you and encourage you along the way.

Remember who you are, what you stand for and who you represent. One day when your journey is complete the greatest words you will hear are, "Well done my good and faithful servant. Come and share in your Master's happiness."

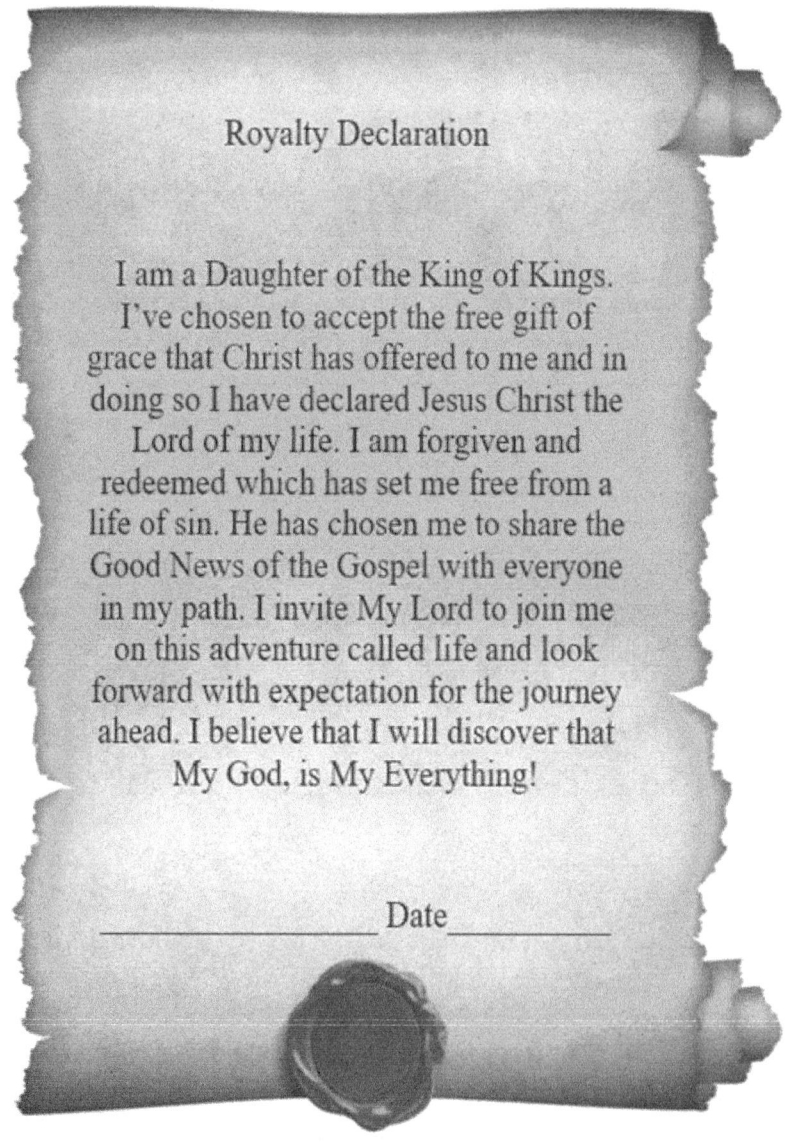

Royalty Declaration

I am a Daughter of the King of Kings. I've chosen to accept the free gift of grace that Christ has offered to me and in doing so I have declared Jesus Christ the Lord of my life. I am forgiven and redeemed which has set me free from a life of sin. He has chosen me to share the Good News of the Gospel with everyone in my path. I invite My Lord to join me on this adventure called life and look forward with expectation for the journey ahead. I believe that I will discover that My God, is My Everything!

_____ Date_____

BE INTENTIONAL

What does it mean to be intentional? By definition it means to do something on purpose. On our daily journey we have endless opportunities to be intentional. We can choose to be intentional about:

- what and who we worship
- how we pray
- how we study the Bible
- our gratitude
- our relationships with God and others.

Being mindful of the many choices we have each day gives us a road map that through the guidance of the Holy Spirit will lead us in discovering God's purpose for our lives.

Being intentional about praying continually will not only connect us more deeply to God, but it will open the pathway of communication to also receive clear direction from Him. Praying with expectation helps us to believe in the promises of God and gives us His peace that surpasses understanding.

Being intentional about knowing His word, not just reading it, will open our lives to the many hidden treasures along the way. We will begin to discover the countless characteristics of God, our lifelong traveling companion. His word is our ultimate travel guide in our journey of life.

Being intentional about gratitude will open our hearts to His continual presence in our lives. As we give thanks - regardless of our feelings, He gives us joy - regardless of our circumstances.

Being intentional about our relationship with God will transform us from being unschooled and ordinary to strong and courageous believers who can do all things through Christ who strengthens us. People will see that we have spent time with Him and have become forever changed.

Being intentional about our relationships with others gives us the opportunity to serve our purpose - to love God and love others. Relationships are a gift from God.

As a believer, being intentional shows faith that God will supply all we need as we freely pour out all we have to others.

The harvest is plentiful and the Lord is asking, "Whom shall I send?" Are you a willing vessel? Do you know that He highly values you and equips you for this calling?

Did you know that there is an abundant need in this world for your exact contribution....your thoughts, your words, your talents.....your exact kind of beautiful!

YES, YOU MATTER GREATLY TO GOD!

You are fearfully and wonderfully made by the Creator of the Universe and you have been given the opportunity to live out that truth.

KNOW IT. BELIEVE IT. LIVE IT.
YOU MATTER!

You matter to God.

Your life matters to God.

Your pain matters to God.

Your sorrow matters to God.

Your joy matters to God.

Your hopes matter to God.

Your questions matter to God.

Your concerns matter to God.

Your suffering matters to God.

You are valuable!

You have influence!

You can do anything!

You are appreciated!

You are loved!

You are talented!

You make a difference!

You are amazing!

YOU ARE A DAUGHTER OF THE KING!

You being right here right now means that you have something to offer. God isn't finished with you so never let anyone, even your own self, tell you that you have nothing to offer or that you are nothing

ACCORDING TO GOD
YOU WERE WORTH DYING FOR.

MY DAILY BREAD

When Jesus' disciples asked Him to teach them how to pray, He responded with what is now called the Lord's Prayer, found in Matthew 6:9-13. He also declared, "I AM the bread of life. Whoever comes to me will never go hungry and whoever believes in me will never be thirsty." (John 6:35)

In the Old Testament God provided manna for the children of Israel one day at a time. Each day as they trusted in God's provision, they would gather what was required and if they gathered more than needed, it would rot.

Every day we have the opportunity to see our tasks, our to-do lists, our relationships and our schedules as daily bread from God. Whatever the day brings we can know with assurance that He has already provided all that we will need to see it through.

God's provision comes in both material and spiritual ways. Perhaps you need actual food, He will provide. Maybe you need patience and grace, He will provide. God is fully aware of everything that will take place today and has already provided all that will be needed.

Our Father in heaven,
Hallowed be Your name.
Your kingdom come,
Your will be done,
on earth as it is in heaven.
Give us this day our daily bread
and forgive us our debts,
as we forgive our debtors.
And lead us not into temptation
but deliver us from the evil one.
For Yours is the kingdom and the power and the glory forever. Amen.

GODLY CHARACTER

As we journey on the paths of our lives, we are given many opportunities to develop Godly character. Each day the Lord orchestrates activities, encounters, allows trials and provides ways out of temptations all of which will help refine us to become all that He created us to be.

When we choose to see these events as learning opportunities and divine encounters, we are better able to respond in ways that reveal the fruit that God's Holy Spirit is producing in us. Galatians 5:22-23 tells us that the fruit of the Spirit is love, joy, peace, patience, kindness, goodness, faithfulness, gentleness and self-control. We are all capable of developing these Godly characteristics in our lives and the more we exercise them, the more they will increase.

Godly character begins with knowing who God is and then living each day in a relationship with Him as He refines us and makes us more like Jesus. It's in the refining that our new character is revealed and our lives begin to reflect the Godly characteristics within. By our fruits the world will know that we are Daughters of The King!

This planner is designed to help you see God's presence, provision, guidance and love throughout your journey, wherever your path may lead. Everything He gives you to do…..He provides a way to be done. Seeing each day as your Daily Bread from God will help you to address situations with Godly character and will help you see God's active presence in your daily life.

As encouragement along the way, you can read the daily blog found at www.mygodmyeverything.org. It will share bible passages, relatable stories and situations as well as Divine Encounters provided by God.

Join me on this journey of discovering that Jesus is our Daily Bread - our portion and all that we need.

ADD THE COLOR

When Jesus spoke again to the people, he said, "I am the
light of the world. Whoever follows me will never walk in
darkness, but will have the light of life." - John 8:12

This world can be a dark place and as Daughters of The King we are called to be a light in the darkness. Godly character adds color to our lives and each fruit of the spirit (love, joy, peace, patience, kindness, goodness, faithfulness and self-control) that is displayed in our lives has the power to brighten not just our path, but the lives and paths of others.

Black and white images give us a basic idea of the scene, but when color is added the picture comes alive and draws us in with a desire to personally experience the image for ourselves.

Everyday life paints a picture and we have the privilege to add the color. We get to love unconditionally. We get to shout for joy because of our Savior. We get to experience peace that transcends understanding. We get to offer the same patience that God grants to us. We get to be kind because we've received kindness. We get to choose goodness to honor our commitment to Christ. We get to remain faithful because He is faithful. We get to share the Good News with gentleness and respect and we get to practice self-control because we love and serve the One who is truly in control.

As Daughters of The King our lives are on display for all to see. Are you living in black and white or are the colors of God's character revealing the light and life that dwells within you? Is your personal relationship with Christ a beautiful scene that others would want to experience for themselves?

"Here's another way to put it: You're here to be light, bringing out the God-colors in the world. God is not a secret to be kept. We're going public with this, as public as a city on a hill. If I make you light-bearers, you don't think I'm going to hide you under a bucket, do you? I'm putting you on a light stand. Now that I've put you there on a hilltop, on a light stand—shine!" - Matthew 5:16 MSG

JESUS IS THE WAY

JESUS IS THE WAY

Jesus answered, "I am the way and the truth and the life.
No one comes to the Father except through me."

Since the beginning of time people have basically been searching for three things: Some direction (the way), something that is real (the truth), and something that will last forever (life.)

In our world there are many ways to travel: highways, back roads, buses, trains, planes and more. The world tells us that there are also many ways, or paths, to reach God: Be a good person, follow a list of do's and don'ts, and go to church and countless different religions. They also say we should do whatever feels best to us, do whatever is right in our own eyes. But the Bible tells us that there is a way that seems right to a man, but in its end is the way to death. (Proverbs 14:12)

The world says the road is wide open and you get to choose which path is right for you to get to God. But the Bible says we should enter by the narrow gate; for wide is the gate and broad is the way that leads to destruction, and there are many who enter through it. Jesus did not tell His disciples about the way or show them the way or guide them along the way, but He said, *"I am the way."*

It's only through Jesus. He is the only way to get saved, to get right with God, and to be born again. If you declare with your mouth, "Jesus is Lord," and believe in your heart that God raised him from the dead, you will be saved. For it is with your heart that you believe and are justified, and it is with your mouth that you profess your faith and are saved. For it is by grace you have been saved, through faith—and this is not from yourselves, it is the gift of God— not by works, so that no one can boast.

God is always present, whispering into our souls and speaking to our hearts. He is there when we are angry, confused, scared, running from Him and too busy for Him. He is the only way we will experience grace, peace, love and hope in this ever searching world.

BREAD FOR YOUR JOURNEY
JESUS IS THE WAY

Jesus answered, "I am the way and the truth and the life.
No one comes to the Father except through me."

John 14:6

Jesus is the stone the builders rejected, which has become the corner-
stone. Salvation is found in no one else, for there is no other name
under heaven given to mankind by which we must be saved.

Acts 4:11-12

If you declare with your mouth, "Jesus is Lord," and believe in your
heart that God raised him from the dead, you will be saved. For it
is with your heart that you believe and are justified, and it is with
your mouth that you profess your faith and are saved. As Scripture
says, "Anyone who believes in him will never be put to shame."

Romans 10:9-11

For it is by grace you have been saved, through faith—and this is not
from yourselves, it is the gift of God— not by works, so that no one
can boast. For we are God's workmanship, created in Christ Jesus
to do good works, which God prepared in advance for us to do.

Ephesians 2:8-10

For God so loved the world that he gave his one and only Son, that
whoever believes in him shall not perish but have eternal life.

John 3:16

My Daily Bread

Date:_____

Everything He gives me to do..............He's already provided a way to be done!

Opportunity Given	Provision Provided
_____	_____
_____	_____
_____	_____
_____	_____

Your will be done. Praises & Prayers

Answered

_____ _____

_____ _____

_____ _____

_____ _____

Forgive me as I forgive others.

_____

_____

_____

Character building moments in my refining process.

_____

_____

_____

Filter my feelings through the truth of Your Word.

_____

_____

This is the day that the Lord has made......I will rejoice and be glad in it!

My Daily Bread

Date:_____

Everything He gives me to do..............He's already provided a way to be done!

Opportunity Given	Provision Provided
_____	_____
_____	_____
_____	_____
_____	_____

Your will be done. Praises & Prayers

Answered

_____   _____

_____   _____

_____   _____

_____   _____

Forgive me as I forgive others.

_____

_____

_____

Character building moments in my refining process.

_____

_____

_____

Filter my feelings through the truth of Your Word.

_____

_____

This is the day that the Lord has made......I will rejoice and be glad in it!

My Daily Bread

Date:_____

Everything He gives me to do..............He's already provided a way to be done!

Opportunity Given	Provision Provided
_____	_____
_____	_____
_____	_____
_____	_____

Your will be done. Praises & Prayers

Answered

____ _____
____ _____
____ _____
____ _____

Forgive me as I forgive others.

_____
_____
_____

Character building moments in my refining process.

_____
_____
_____

Filter my feelings through the truth of Your Word.

_____
_____

This is the day that the Lord has made......I will rejoice and be glad in it!

My Daily Bread   Date:_____

Everything He gives me to do..............He's already provided a way to be done!

Opportunity Given	Provision Provided
_____	_____
_____	_____
_____	_____
_____	_____

Your will be done. Praises & Prayers

Answered

_____   _____

_____   _____

_____   _____

_____   _____

Forgive me as I forgive others.

_____

_____

_____

Character building moments in my refining process.

_____

_____

_____

Filter my feelings through the truth of Your Word.

_____

_____

This is the day that the Lord has made......I will rejoice and be glad in it!

My Daily Bread

Date:_____

Everything He gives me to do..............He's already provided a way to be done!

Opportunity Given	Provision Provided
_____	_____
_____	_____
_____	_____
_____	_____

Your will be done. Praises & Prayers

Answered

_____ _____

_____ _____

_____ _____

_____ _____

Forgive me as I forgive others.

_____

_____

_____

Character building moments in my refining process.

_____

_____

_____

Filter my feelings through the truth of Your Word.

_____

_____

This is the day that the Lord has made......I will rejoice and be glad in it!

My Daily Bread

Date:_____

Everything He gives me to do..............He's already provided a way to be done!

Opportunity Given	Provision Provided
_____	_____
_____	_____
_____	_____
_____	_____

Your will be done. Praises & Prayers

Answered

_____ _____

_____ _____

_____ _____

_____ _____

Forgive me as I forgive others.

_____

_____

_____

Character building moments in my refining process.

_____

_____

_____

Filter my feelings through the truth of Your Word.

_____

_____

This is the day that the Lord has made......I will rejoice and be glad in it!

My Daily Bread

Date:_____

Everything He gives me to do..............He's already provided a way to be done!

Opportunity Given	Provision Provided
_____	_____
_____	_____
_____	_____
_____	_____

Your will be done. Praises & Prayers

Answered

_____ _____

_____ _____

_____ _____

_____ _____

Forgive me as I forgive others.

_____

_____

_____

Character building moments in my refining process.

_____

_____

_____

Filter my feelings through the truth of Your Word.

_____

_____

This is the day that the Lord has made......I will rejoice and be glad in it!

My Daily Bread

Date:_____

Everything He gives me to do...............He's already provided a way to be done!

Opportunity Given	Provision Provided
_____	_____
_____	_____
_____	_____
_____	_____

Your will be done. Praises & Prayers

Answered

_____ _____

_____ _____

_____ _____

_____ _____

Forgive me as I forgive others.

Character building moments in my refining process.

Filter my feelings through the truth of Your Word.

This is the day that the Lord has made......I will rejoice and be glad in it!

My Daily Bread

Date:_____

Everything He gives me to do..............He's already provided a way to be done!

Opportunity Given	Provision Provided
_____	_____
_____	_____
_____	_____
_____	_____

Your will be done. Praises & Prayers

Answered

_____ _____
_____ _____
_____ _____
_____ _____

Forgive me as I forgive others.

_____
_____
_____

Character building moments in my refining process.

_____
_____
_____

Filter my feelings through the truth of Your Word.

_____
_____

This is the day that the Lord has made......I will rejoice and be glad in it!

My Daily Bread

Date:_____

Everything He gives me to do..............He's already provided a way to be done!

Opportunity Given	Provision Provided
_____	_____
_____	_____
_____	_____
_____	_____

Your will be done. Praises & Prayers

Answered

_____ _____

_____ _____

_____ _____

_____ _____

Forgive me as I forgive others.

_____

_____

_____

Character building moments in my refining process.

_____

_____

_____

Filter my feelings through the truth of Your Word.

_____

_____

This is the day that the Lord has made.......I will rejoice and be glad in it!

My Daily Bread

Date:_____

Everything He gives me to do..............He's already provided a way to be done!

Opportunity Given	Provision Provided
_____	_____
_____	_____
_____	_____
_____	_____

Your will be done. Praises & Prayers

Answered

_____ _____

_____ _____

_____ _____

_____ _____

Forgive me as I forgive others.

_____
_____
_____

Character building moments in my refining process.

_____
_____
_____

Filter my feelings through the truth of Your Word.

_____
_____

This is the day that the Lord has made......I will rejoice and be glad in it!

My Daily Bread

Date:_____

Everything He gives me to do..............He's already provided a way to be done!

Opportunity Given	Provision Provided
_____	_____
_____	_____
_____	_____
_____	_____

Your will be done. Praises & Prayers

Answered

_____ _____

_____ _____

_____ _____

_____ _____

Forgive me as I forgive others.

_____
_____
_____

Character building moments in my refining process.

_____
_____
_____

Filter my feelings through the truth of Your Word.

_____
_____

This is the day that the Lord has made......I will rejoice and be glad in it!

My Daily Bread

Date:_____

Everything He gives me to do..............He's already provided a way to be done!

Opportunity Given	Provision Provided
_____	_____
_____	_____
_____	_____
_____	_____

Your will be done. Praises & Prayers

Answered

____ _____
____ _____
____ _____
____ _____

Forgive me as I forgive others.

_____
_____
_____
_____

Character building moments in my refining process.

_____
_____
_____

Filter my feelings through the truth of Your Word.

_____
_____

This is the day that the Lord has made......I will rejoice and be glad in it!

My Daily Bread

Date:_____

Everything He gives me to do..............He's already provided a way to be done!

Opportunity Given	Provision Provided
_____	_____
_____	_____
_____	_____
_____	_____

Your will be done. Praises & Prayers

Answered

_____ _____

_____ _____

_____ _____

_____ _____

Forgive me as I forgive others.

_____

_____

_____

Character building moments in my refining process.

_____

_____

_____

Filter my feelings through the truth of Your Word.

_____

_____

This is the day that the Lord has made......I will rejoice and be glad in it!

My Daily Bread

Date:_____

Everything He gives me to do..............He's already provided a way to be done!

Opportunity Given	Provision Provided
_____	_____
_____	_____
_____	_____
_____	_____

Your will be done. Praises & Prayers

Answered

_____	_____
_____	_____
_____	_____
_____	_____

Forgive me as I forgive others.

_____
_____
_____

Character building moments in my refining process.

_____
_____
_____

Filter my feelings through the truth of Your Word.

_____
_____

This is the day that the Lord has made......I will rejoice and be glad in it!

My Daily Bread

Date:_____

Everything He gives me to do..............He's already provided a way to be done!

Opportunity Given	Provision Provided
_____	_____
_____	_____
_____	_____
_____	_____

Your will be done. Praises & Prayers

Answered

_____	_____
_____	_____
_____	_____
_____	_____

Forgive me as I forgive others.

_____
_____
_____

Character building moments in my refining process.

_____
_____
_____

Filter my feelings through the truth of Your Word.

_____
_____

This is the day that the Lord has made.......I will rejoice and be glad in it!

My Daily Bread

Date:_____

Everything He gives me to do..............He's already provided a way to be done!

Opportunity Given	Provision Provided
_____	_____
_____	_____
_____	_____
_____	_____

Your will be done. Praises & Prayers

Answered

Forgive me as I forgive others.

Character building moments in my refining process.

Filter my feelings through the truth of Your Word.

This is the day that the Lord has made......I will rejoice and be glad in it!

My Daily Bread

Date:_____

Everything He gives me to do..............He's already provided a way to be done!

Opportunity Given   Provision Provided

_____   _____

_____   _____

_____   _____

_____   _____

Your will be done. Praises & Prayers

Answered

_____   _____

_____   _____

_____   _____

_____   _____

Forgive me as I forgive others.

_____

_____

_____

Character building moments in my refining process.

_____

_____

_____

Filter my feelings through the truth of Your Word.

_____

_____

This is the day that the Lord has made......I will rejoice and be glad in it!

My Daily Bread

Date:_____

Everything He gives me to do..............He's already provided a way to be done!

Opportunity Given	Provision Provided
_____	_____
_____	_____
_____	_____
_____	_____

Your will be done. Praises & Prayers

Answered

_____ _____
_____ _____
_____ _____
_____ _____

Forgive me as I forgive others.

_____
_____
_____

Character building moments in my refining process.

_____
_____
_____

Filter my feelings through the truth of Your Word.

_____
_____

This is the day that the Lord has made......I will rejoice and be glad in it!

My Daily Bread

Date:_____

Everything He gives me to do..............He's already provided a way to be done!

Opportunity Given	Provision Provided
_____	_____
_____	_____
_____	_____
_____	_____

Your will be done. Praises & Prayers

Answered

_____ _____

_____ _____

_____ _____

_____ _____

Forgive me as I forgive others.

_____

_____

_____

Character building moments in my refining process.

_____

_____

_____

Filter my feelings through the truth of Your Word.

_____

_____

This is the day that the Lord has made......I will rejoice and be glad in it!

My Daily Bread

Date:_____

Everything He gives me to do..............He's already provided a way to be done!

Opportunity Given	Provision Provided
_____	_____
_____	_____
_____	_____
_____	_____

Your will be done. Praises & Prayers

Answered

_____ _____

_____ _____

_____ _____

_____ _____

Forgive me as I forgive others.

_____

_____

_____

Character building moments in my refining process.

_____

_____

_____

Filter my feelings through the truth of Your Word.

_____

_____

This is the day that the Lord has made......I will rejoice and be glad in it!

My Daily Bread

Everything He gives me to do..............He's already provided a way to be done!

Opportunity Given	Provision Provided
_____	_____
_____	_____
_____	_____
_____	_____

Your will be done. Praises & Prayers

Answered

_____ _____
_____ _____
_____ _____
_____ _____

Forgive me as I forgive others.

_____
_____
_____

Character building moments in my refining process.

_____
_____
_____

Filter my feelings through the truth of Your Word.

_____
_____

This is the day that the Lord has made......I will rejoice and be glad in it!

My Daily Bread

Date:_____

Everything He gives me to do..............He's already provided a way to be done!

Opportunity Given   Provision Provided

_____   _____

_____   _____

_____   _____

_____   _____

Your will be done. Praises & Prayers

Answered

_____   _____

_____   _____

_____   _____

_____   _____

Forgive me as I forgive others.

_____

_____

_____

Character building moments in my refining process.

_____

_____

_____

Filter my feelings through the truth of Your Word.

_____

_____

This is the day that the Lord has made......I will rejoice and be glad in it!

My Daily Bread

Date:_____

Everything He gives me to do..............He's already provided a way to be done!

Opportunity Given	Provision Provided
_____	_____
_____	_____
_____	_____
_____	_____

Your will be done. Praises & Prayers

Answered

_____   _____
_____   _____
_____   _____
_____   _____

Forgive me as I forgive others.

_____
_____
_____

Character building moments in my refining process.

_____
_____
_____

Filter my feelings through the truth of Your Word.

_____
_____

This is the day that the Lord has made......I will rejoice and be glad in it!

My Daily Bread

Date:_____

Everything He gives me to do..............He's already provided a way to be done!

Opportunity Given	Provision Provided
_____	_____
_____	_____
_____	_____
_____	_____

Your will be done. Praises & Prayers

Answered

Forgive me as I forgive others.

Character building moments in my refining process.

Filter my feelings through the truth of Your Word.

This is the day that the Lord has made......I will rejoice and be glad in it!

My Daily Bread

Date:_____

Everything He gives me to do..............He's already provided a way to be done!

Opportunity Given	Provision Provided
_____	_____
_____	_____
_____	_____
_____	_____

Your will be done. Praises & Prayers

Answered

_____	_____
_____	_____
_____	_____
_____	_____

Forgive me as I forgive others.

Character building moments in my refining process.

Filter my feelings through the truth of Your Word.

This is the day that the Lord has made......I will rejoice and be glad in it!

My Daily Bread

Date:_____

Everything He gives me to do..............He's already provided a way to be done!

Opportunity Given	Provision Provided
_____	_____
_____	_____
_____	_____
_____	_____

Your will be done. Praises & Prayers

Answered

_____ _____

_____ _____

_____ _____

_____ _____

Forgive me as I forgive others.

_____

_____

_____

Character building moments in my refining process.

_____

_____

_____

Filter my feelings through the truth of Your Word.

_____

_____

This is the day that the Lord has made......I will rejoice and be glad in it!

My Daily Bread

Date:_____

Everything He gives me to do..............He's already provided a way to be done!

Opportunity Given	Provision Provided
_____	_____
_____	_____
_____	_____
_____	_____

Your will be done. Praises & Prayers

Answered

____ _____
____ _____
____ _____
____ _____

Forgive me as I forgive others.

_____
_____
_____

Character building moments in my refining process.

_____
_____
_____

Filter my feelings through the truth of Your Word.

_____
_____

This is the day that the Lord has made......I will rejoice and be glad in it!

My Daily Bread

Date:_____

Everything He gives me to do..............He's already provided a way to be done!

Opportunity Given	Provision Provided
_____	_____
_____	_____
_____	_____
_____	_____

Your will be done. Praises & Prayers

Answered

_____ _____

_____ _____

_____ _____

_____ _____

Forgive me as I forgive others.

Character building moments in my refining process.

Filter my feelings through the truth of Your Word.

This is the day that the Lord has made......I will rejoice and be glad in it!

My Daily Bread

Date:_____

Everything He gives me to do..............He's already provided a way to be done!

Opportunity Given	Provision Provided
_____	_____
_____	_____
_____	_____
_____	_____

Your will be done. Praises & Prayers

Answered

_____	_____
_____	_____
_____	_____
_____	_____

Forgive me as I forgive others.

_____

_____

_____

Character building moments in my refining process.

_____

_____

Filter my feelings through the truth of Your Word.

_____

_____

This is the day that the Lord has made......I will rejoice and be glad in it!

My Daily Bread

Everything He gives me to do..............He's already provided a way to be done!

Opportunity Given	Provision Provided
_____	_____
_____	_____
_____	_____
_____	_____

Your will be done. Praises & Prayers

Answered

_____ _____
_____ _____
_____ _____
_____ _____

Forgive me as I forgive others.

_____
_____
_____

Character building moments in my refining process.

_____
_____
_____

Filter my feelings through the truth of Your Word.

_____
_____

This is the day that the Lord has made......I will rejoice and be glad in it!

JESUS IS THE TRUTH

JESUS IS THE TRUTH

Now more than ever we want to know the truth. We are tired of the phony, misleading, fake and outright lies that we are constantly fed by this world. We want something that is genuine, reliable and trustworthy.

Jesus said, "I am the way and the truth."

Centuries ago Pilate asked Jesus, "What is truth?" The answer was standing before him - Jesus is truth. Just as Pilate's view was focused only on his present circumstances, we too can be blinded by the troubles we face and be completely unaware of the truth that is right in front of us. Thankfully we have God's word, the Bible, which reveals to everyone who is willing to see with their eyes and hear with their ears, God's revelation of truth.

The Truth tells us that He will never leave us nor forsake us which means that although it may seem we face our giants alone, Jesus is right beside us fighting our battles.

The Truth tells us that in this world we will have troubles but to take heart because He has overcome the world and He is close to the brokenhearted and saves those who are crushed in spirit. One day He will wipe away every tear.

The Truth tells us that He loves us with an everlasting love and because of that love He endured the cross and by His stripes we are seat free. Then He rose from the grave, conquering sin and death and is preparing a place for us. He is making all things new.

When we read and properly apply God's word we can see the real truth of our circumstances from God's perspective and find the encouragement, wisdom and hope that come with trusting the One who is Truth.

BREAD FOR YOUR JOURNEY
JESUS IS THE TRUTH

God has said, "Never will I leave you; never will I forsake you."

Hebrews 13:5

I have told you these things, so that in me you may have peace. In this world you will have trouble. But take heart! I have overcome the world.

John 16:33

The Lord is close to the brokenhearted and saves those who are crushed in spirit.

Psalm 34:18

I have loved you with an everlasting love; I have drawn you with unfailing kindness.

Jeremiah 31:3

But he was pierced for our transgressions, he was crushed for our iniquities; the punishment that brought us peace was on him, and by his wounds we are healed.

Isaiah 53:5

He will wipe away every tear from their eyes, and death shall be no more, neither shall there be mourning, nor crying, nor pain anymore, for the former things have passed away. He who was seated on the throne said, "I am making everything new!" Then he said, "Write this down, for these words are trustworthy and true."

Revelation 21:4-5

My Daily Bread

Date:_____

Everything He gives me to do..............He's already provided a way to be done!

Opportunity Given	Provision Provided
_____	_____
_____	_____
_____	_____
_____	_____

Your will be done. Praises & Prayers

Answered

____ _____

____ _____

____ _____

____ _____

Forgive me as I forgive others.

_____

_____

_____

Character building moments in my refining process.

_____

_____

_____

Filter my feelings through the truth of Your Word.

_____

_____

This is the day that the Lord has made......I will rejoice and be glad in it!

My Daily Bread

Date:_____

Everything He gives me to do..............He's already provided a way to be done!

Opportunity Given	Provision Provided
_____	_____
_____	_____
_____	_____
_____	_____

Your will be done. Praises & Prayers

Answered

_____ | _____
_____ | _____
_____ | _____
_____ | _____

Forgive me as I forgive others.

_____
_____
_____
_____

Character building moments in my refining process.

_____
_____
_____

Filter my feelings through the truth of Your Word.

_____
_____

This is the day that the Lord has made......I will rejoice and be glad in it!

My Daily Bread

Date:_____

Everything He gives me to do..............He's already provided a way to be done!

Opportunity Given	Provision Provided
_____	_____
_____	_____
_____	_____
_____	_____

Your will be done. Praises & Prayers

Answered

Forgive me as I forgive others.

Character building moments in my refining process.

Filter my feelings through the truth of Your Word.

This is the day that the Lord has made......I will rejoice and be glad in it!

My Daily Bread

Date:_____

Everything He gives me to do..............He's already provided a way to be done!

Opportunity Given	Provision Provided
_____	_____
_____	_____
_____	_____
_____	_____

Your will be done. Praises & Prayers

Answered

Forgive me as I forgive others.

Character building moments in my refining process.

Filter my feelings through the truth of Your Word.

This is the day that the Lord has made......I will rejoice and be glad in it!

My Daily Bread

Date:_____

Everything He gives me to do..............He's already provided a way to be done!

Opportunity Given	Provision Provided
_____	_____
_____	_____
_____	_____
_____	_____

Your will be done. Praises & Prayers

Answered

_____ _____

_____ _____

_____ _____

_____ _____

Forgive me as I forgive others.

_____

_____

_____

Character building moments in my refining process.

_____

_____

_____

Filter my feelings through the truth of Your Word.

_____

_____

This is the day that the Lord has made......I will rejoice and be glad in it!

My Daily Bread

Date:_____

Everything He gives me to do..............He's already provided a way to be done!

Opportunity Given	Provision Provided
_____	_____
_____	_____
_____	_____
_____	_____

Your will be done. Praises & Prayers

Answered

Forgive me as I forgive others.

Character building moments in my refining process.

Filter my feelings through the truth of Your Word.

This is the day that the Lord has made......I will rejoice and be glad in it!

My Daily Bread

Date:_____

Everything He gives me to do..............He's already provided a way to be done!

Opportunity Given	Provision Provided
_____	_____
_____	_____
_____	_____
_____	_____

Your will be done. Praises & Prayers

Answered

____ _____
____ _____
____ _____
____ _____

Forgive me as I forgive others.

Character building moments in my refining process.

Filter my feelings through the truth of Your Word.

This is the day that the Lord has made......I will rejoice and be glad in it!

My Daily Bread

Date:_____

Everything He gives me to do..............He's already provided a way to be done!

Opportunity Given	Provision Provided
_____	_____
_____	_____
_____	_____
_____	_____

Your will be done. Praises & Prayers

Answered

_____ _____
_____ _____
_____ _____
_____ _____

Forgive me as I forgive others.

_____
_____
_____

Character building moments in my refining process.

_____
_____
_____

Filter my feelings through the truth of Your Word.

_____
_____

This is the day that the Lord has made......I will rejoice and be glad in it!

My Daily Bread

Date:_____

Everything He gives me to do..............He's already provided a way to be done!

Opportunity Given　　　　　　　　　　　　Provision Provided

_____　　　　　_____

_____　　　　　_____

_____　　　　　_____

_____　　　　　_____

Your will be done. Praises & Prayers

Answered

_____　_____

_____　_____

_____　_____

_____　_____

Forgive me as I forgive others.

_____

_____

_____

Character building moments in my refining process.

_____

_____

_____

Filter my feelings through the truth of Your Word.

_____

_____

This is the day that the Lord has made......I will rejoice and be glad in it!

My Daily Bread

Date:_____

Everything He gives me to do..............He's already provided a way to be done!

Opportunity Given	Provision Provided
_____	_____
_____	_____
_____	_____
_____	_____

Your will be done. Praises & Prayers

Answered

_____ _____

_____ _____

_____ _____

_____ _____

Forgive me as I forgive others.

_____

_____

_____

Character building moments in my refining process.

_____

_____

_____

Filter my feelings through the truth of Your Word.

_____

_____

This is the day that the Lord has made......I will rejoice and be glad in it!

My Daily Bread

Date:_____

Everything He gives me to do..............He's already provided a way to be done!

Opportunity Given	Provision Provided
_____	_____
_____	_____
_____	_____
_____	_____

Your will be done. Praises & Prayers

Answered

Forgive me as I forgive others.

Character building moments in my refining process.

Filter my feelings through the truth of Your Word.

This is the day that the Lord has made......I will rejoice and be glad in it!

My Daily Bread

Date:_____

Everything He gives me to do..............He's already provided a way to be done!

Opportunity Given	Provision Provided
_____	_____
_____	_____
_____	_____
_____	_____

Your will be done. Praises & Prayers

Answered

_____ _____

_____ _____

_____ _____

_____ _____

Forgive me as I forgive others.

_____

_____

_____

Character building moments in my refining process.

_____

_____

_____

Filter my feelings through the truth of Your Word.

_____

_____

This is the day that the Lord has made......I will rejoice and be glad in it!

My Daily Bread

Date:_____

Everything He gives me to do..............He's already provided a way to be done!

Opportunity Given	Provision Provided
_____	_____
_____	_____
_____	_____
_____	_____

Your will be done. Praises & Prayers

Answered

_____ _____

_____ _____

_____ _____

_____ _____

Forgive me as I forgive others.

_____
_____
_____

Character building moments in my refining process.

_____
_____
_____

Filter my feelings through the truth of Your Word.

_____
_____

This is the day that the Lord has made......I will rejoice and be glad in it!

My Daily Bread   Date:_____

Everything He gives me to do..............He's already provided a way to be done!

Opportunity Given	Provision Provided
_____	_____
_____	_____
_____	_____
_____	_____

Your will be done. Praises & Prayers

Answered
_____   _____
_____   _____
_____   _____
_____   _____

Forgive me as I forgive others.

_____
_____
_____

Character building moments in my refining process.

_____
_____
_____

Filter my feelings through the truth of Your Word.

_____
_____

This is the day that the Lord has made......I will rejoice and be glad in it!

My Daily Bread

Date:_____

Everything He gives me to do..............He's already provided a way to be done!

Opportunity Given	Provision Provided
_____	_____
_____	_____
_____	_____
_____	_____

Your will be done. Praises & Prayers

Answered

_____ _____
_____ _____
_____ _____
_____ _____

Forgive me as I forgive others.

_____
_____
_____

Character building moments in my refining process.

_____
_____
_____

Filter my feelings through the truth of Your Word.

_____
_____

This is the day that the Lord has made......I will rejoice and be glad in it!

My Daily Bread

Everything He gives me to do..............He's already provided a way to be done!

Opportunity Given	Provision Provided

Your will be done. Praises & Prayers

Answered

Forgive me as I forgive others.

Character building moments in my refining process.

Filter my feelings through the truth of Your Word.

This is the day that the Lord has made......I will rejoice and be glad in it!

My Daily Bread

Date:_____

Everything He gives me to do..............He's already provided a way to be done!

Opportunity Given   Provision Provided

_____   _____

_____   _____

_____   _____

_____   _____

Your will be done. Praises & Prayers

Answered

_____ _____

_____ _____

_____ _____

_____ _____

Forgive me as I forgive others.

_____

_____

_____

_____

Character building moments in my refining process.

_____

_____

_____

Filter my feelings through the truth of Your Word.

_____

_____

This is the day that the Lord has made......I will rejoice and be glad in it!

My Daily Bread

Date:_____

Everything He gives me to do..............He's already provided a way to be done!

Opportunity Given	Provision Provided
_____	_____
_____	_____
_____	_____
_____	_____

Your will be done. Praises & Prayers

Answered

_____ _____
_____ _____
_____ _____
_____ _____

Forgive me as I forgive others.

Character building moments in my refining process.

Filter my feelings through the truth of Your Word.

This is the day that the Lord has made......I will rejoice and be glad in it!

My Daily Bread

Date:_____

Everything He gives me to do..............He's already provided a way to be done!

Opportunity Given	Provision Provided
_____	_____
_____	_____
_____	_____
_____	_____

Your will be done. Praises & Prayers

Answered

_____ _____
_____ _____
_____ _____
_____ _____

Forgive me as I forgive others.

_____
_____
_____

Character building moments in my refining process.

_____
_____
_____

Filter my feelings through the truth of Your Word.

_____
_____

This is the day that the Lord has made......I will rejoice and be glad in it!

My Daily Bread

Date:_____

Everything He gives me to do..............He's already provided a way to be done!

Opportunity Given	Provision Provided
_____	_____
_____	_____
_____	_____
_____	_____

Your will be done. Praises & Prayers

Answered

_____ _____
_____ _____
_____ _____
_____ _____

Forgive me as I forgive others.

_____
_____
_____

Character building moments in my refining process.

_____
_____
_____

Filter my feelings through the truth of Your Word.

_____
_____

This is the day that the Lord has made......I will rejoice and be glad in it!

My Daily Bread

Date:_____

Everything He gives me to do...............He's already provided a way to be done!

Opportunity Given	Provision Provided
_____	_____
_____	_____
_____	_____
_____	_____

Your will be done. Praises & Prayers

Answered

_____ _____

_____ _____

_____ _____

_____ _____

Forgive me as I forgive others.

Character building moments in my refining process.

Filter my feelings through the truth of Your Word.

This is the day that the Lord has made......I will rejoice and be glad in it!

My Daily Bread

Date:_____

Everything He gives me to do..............He's already provided a way to be done!

Opportunity Given	Provision Provided
_____	_____
_____	_____
_____	_____
_____	_____

Your will be done. Praises & Prayers

Answered

Forgive me as I forgive others.

Character building moments in my refining process.

Filter my feelings through the truth of Your Word.

This is the day that the Lord has made......I will rejoice and be glad in it!

My Daily Bread

Date:_____

Everything He gives me to do..............He's already provided a way to be done!

Opportunity Given   Provision Provided

_____   _____

_____   _____

_____   _____

_____   _____

Your will be done. Praises & Prayers

Answered

_____   _____

_____   _____

_____   _____

_____   _____

Forgive me as I forgive others.

_____

_____

_____

Character building moments in my refining process.

_____

_____

_____

Filter my feelings through the truth of Your Word.

_____

_____

This is the day that the Lord has made......I will rejoice and be glad in it!

My Daily Bread

Date:_____

Everything He gives me to do...............He's already provided a way to be done!

Opportunity Given	Provision Provided
_____	_____
_____	_____
_____	_____
_____	_____

Your will be done. Praises & Prayers

Answered

_____ _____

_____ _____

_____ _____

_____ _____

Forgive me as I forgive others.

_____

_____

_____

Character building moments in my refining process.

_____

_____

_____

Filter my feelings through the truth of Your Word.

_____

_____

This is the day that the Lord has made......I will rejoice and be glad in it!

My Daily Bread

Date:_____

Everything He gives me to do..............He's already provided a way to be done!

Opportunity Given	Provision Provided
_____	_____
_____	_____
_____	_____
_____	_____

Your will be done. Praises & Prayers

Answered

_____

_____

_____

_____

Forgive me as I forgive others.

Character building moments in my refining process.

Filter my feelings through the truth of Your Word.

This is the day that the Lord has made......I will rejoice and be glad in it!

My Daily Bread

Date:_____

Everything He gives me to do...............He's already provided a way to be done!

Opportunity Given	Provision Provided
_____	_____
_____	_____
_____	_____
_____	_____

Your will be done. Praises & Prayers

Answered

_____	_____
_____	_____
_____	_____
_____	_____

Forgive me as I forgive others.

_____
_____
_____

Character building moments in my refining process.

_____
_____
_____

Filter my feelings through the truth of Your Word.

_____
_____

This is the day that the Lord has made......I will rejoice and be glad in it!

My Daily Bread

Date:_____

Everything He gives me to do..............He's already provided a way to be done!

Opportunity Given	Provision Provided
_____	_____
_____	_____
_____	_____
_____	_____

Your will be done. Praises & Prayers

Answered

Forgive me as I forgive others.

Character building moments in my refining process.

Filter my feelings through the truth of Your Word.

This is the day that the Lord has made......I will rejoice and be glad in it!

My Daily Bread

Date:_____

Everything He gives me to do..............He's already provided a way to be done!

Opportunity Given	Provision Provided
_____	_____
_____	_____
_____	_____
_____	_____

Your will be done. Praises & Prayers

Answered

_____ _____
_____ _____
_____ _____
_____ _____

Forgive me as I forgive others.

_____
_____
_____

Character building moments in my refining process.

_____
_____
_____

Filter my feelings through the truth of Your Word.

_____
_____

This is the day that the Lord has made......I will rejoice and be glad in it!

My Daily Bread

Date:_____

Everything He gives me to do...............He's already provided a way to be done!

Opportunity Given　　　　　　　　　　　Provision Provided

_____　　　　_____

_____　　　　_____

_____　　　　_____

_____　　　　_____

Your will be done. Praises & Prayers

Answered

_____　_____

_____　_____

_____　_____

_____　_____

Forgive me as I forgive others.

_____

_____

_____

Character building moments in my refining process.

_____

_____

_____

Filter my feelings through the truth of Your Word.

_____

_____

This is the day that the Lord has made......I will rejoice and be glad in it!

My Daily Bread

Date:_____

Everything He gives me to do..............He's already provided a way to be done!

Opportunity Given	Provision Provided
_____	_____
_____	_____
_____	_____
_____	_____

Your will be done. Praises & Prayers

Answered

_____	_____
_____	_____
_____	_____
_____	_____

Forgive me as I forgive others.

_____
_____
_____

Character building moments in my refining process.

_____
_____
_____

Filter my feelings through the truth of Your Word.

_____
_____

This is the day that the Lord has made.......I will rejoice and be glad in it!

My Daily Bread

Date:_____

Everything He gives me to do.............He's already provided a way to be done!

Opportunity Given	Provision Provided
_____	_____
_____	_____
_____	_____
_____	_____

Your will be done. Praises & Prayers

Answered

_____ _____
_____ _____
_____ _____
_____ _____

Forgive me as I forgive others.

_____
_____
_____

Character building moments in my refining process.

_____
_____
_____

Filter my feelings through the truth of Your Word.

_____
_____

This is the day that the Lord has made......I will rejoice and be glad in it!

JESUS IS THE LIFE

JESUS IS THE LIFE

We have all heard about living the American dream which usually includes a respectable job, nice home, new cars, vacations and the appearance that everything is just perfect. But the truth is that it's just a dream. In time our beauty fades, relationships change and we can lose our jobs, homes, health and money. The storms of life can wash away our dream lives that are built on sand.

Jesus told us in John 10:10, "The thief comes only to steal and kill and destroy; I have come that they may have life, and have it more abundantly." He said, "I am the bread of life, I have the words of life, and whoever finds me finds life, whoever believes in me has eternal life, and whoever believes in me his name will be written down in the lamb's Book of Life." Jesus is eternal and will never end.

As new creations in Christ we have the privilege of living for Him. Our old ways of thinking are gone and replaced with the truth of His word revealing what abundant life really is - who it is.

The apostle Paul described a new life in Christ as follows, "But whatever were gains to me I now consider loss for the sake of Christ. What is more, I consider everything a loss because of the surpassing worth of knowing Christ Jesus my Lord, for whose sake I have lost all things. I consider them garbage, that I may gain Christ and be found in him, not having a righteousness of my own that comes from the law, but that which is through faith in Christ—the righteousness that comes from God on the basis of faith. I want to know Christ—yes, to know the power of his resurrection and participation in his sufferings, becoming like him in his death, and so, somehow, attaining to the resurrection from the dead. Not that I have already obtained all this, or have already arrived at my goal, but I press on to take hold of that for which Christ Jesus took hold of me. (Philippians 3:7-12)

Jesus said, "I am the way, the truth and the life." Everything that we are looking for can be found in Him.

BREAD FOR YOUR JOURNEY
JESUS IS THE LIFE

*I have been crucified with Christ. It is no longer I who live, but
Christ who lives in me. And the life I now live in the flesh I live by
faith in the Son of God, who loved me and gave himself for me.*

Galatians 2:20

*Therefore, if anyone is in Christ, he is a new creation. The
old has passed away; behold, the new has come.*

2 Corinthians 5:17

*Jesus said to her, "I am the resurrection and the life. Whoever
believes in me, though he dies, yet shall he live, and everyone who
lives and believes in me shall never die. Do you believe this?*

John 11:25-26

*The thief comes only to steal and kill and destroy; I have come
that they may have life, and have it more abundantly.*

John 10:10

For those who find me find life and receive favor from the Lord.

Proverbs 8:35

My Daily Bread

Date:_____

Everything He gives me to do..............He's already provided a way to be done!

Opportunity Given	Provision Provided
_____	_____
_____	_____
_____	_____
_____	_____

Your will be done. Praises & Prayers

Answered

_____	_____
_____	_____
_____	_____
_____	_____

Forgive me as I forgive others.

_____
_____
_____

Character building moments in my refining process.

_____
_____
_____

Filter my feelings through the truth of Your Word.

_____
_____

This is the day that the Lord has made......I will rejoice and be glad in it!

My Daily Bread

Date:_____

Everything He gives me to do..............He's already provided a way to be done!

Opportunity Given	Provision Provided
_____	_____
_____	_____
_____	_____
_____	_____

Your will be done. Praises & Prayers

Answered

_____	_____
_____	_____
_____	_____
_____	_____

Forgive me as I forgive others.

_____
_____
_____

Character building moments in my refining process.

_____
_____
_____

Filter my feelings through the truth of Your Word.

_____
_____

This is the day that the Lord has made......I will rejoice and be glad in it!

My Daily Bread

Date:_____

Everything He gives me to do..............He's already provided a way to be done!

Opportunity Given	Provision Provided

Your will be done. Praises & Prayers

Answered

Forgive me as I forgive others.

Character building moments in my refining process.

Filter my feelings through the truth of Your Word.

This is the day that the Lord has made......I will rejoice and be glad in it!

My Daily Bread

Date:_____

Everything He gives me to do..............He's already provided a way to be done!

Opportunity Given	Provision Provided
_____	_____
_____	_____
_____	_____
_____	_____

Your will be done. Praises & Prayers

Answered

_____   _____

_____   _____

_____   _____

_____   _____

Forgive me as I forgive others.

_____

_____

_____

_____

Character building moments in my refining process.

_____

_____

_____

Filter my feelings through the truth of Your Word.

_____

_____

This is the day that the Lord has made......I will rejoice and be glad in it!

My Daily Bread

Date:_____

Everything He gives me to do..............He's already provided a way to be done!

Opportunity Given	Provision Provided
_____	_____
_____	_____
_____	_____
_____	_____

Your will be done. Praises & Prayers

Answered

Forgive me as I forgive others.

Character building moments in my refining process.

Filter my feelings through the truth of Your Word.

This is the day that the Lord has made......I will rejoice and be glad in it!

My Daily Bread

Date:_____

Everything He gives me to do..............He's already provided a way to be done!

Opportunity Given	Provision Provided
_____	_____
_____	_____
_____	_____
_____	_____

Your will be done. Praises & Prayers

Answered

_____ _____

_____ _____

_____ _____

_____ _____

Forgive me as I forgive others.

_____

_____

_____

Character building moments in my refining process.

_____

_____

_____

Filter my feelings through the truth of Your Word.

_____

_____

This is the day that the Lord has made......I will rejoice and be glad in it!

My Daily Bread

Date:_____

Everything He gives me to do..............He's already provided a way to be done!

Opportunity Given	Provision Provided
_____	_____
_____	_____
_____	_____
_____	_____

Your will be done. Praises & Prayers

Answered

____ _____

____ _____

____ _____

____ _____

Forgive me as I forgive others.

_____
_____
_____

Character building moments in my refining process.

_____
_____
_____

Filter my feelings through the truth of Your Word.

_____
_____

This is the day that the Lord has made......I will rejoice and be glad in it!

My Daily Bread

Date:_____

Everything He gives me to do..............He's already provided a way to be done!

Opportunity Given	Provision Provided
_____	_____
_____	_____
_____	_____
_____	_____

Your will be done. Praises & Prayers

Answered

_____ _____

_____ _____

_____ _____

_____ _____

Forgive me as I forgive others.

_____
_____
_____
_____

Character building moments in my refining process.

_____
_____
_____

Filter my feelings through the truth of Your Word.

_____
_____

This is the day that the Lord has made......I will rejoice and be glad in it!

My Daily Bread

Date:_____

Everything He gives me to do..............He's already provided a way to be done!

Opportunity Given	Provision Provided
_____	_____
_____	_____
_____	_____
_____	_____

Your will be done. Praises & Prayers

Answered

_____ _____

_____ _____

_____ _____

_____ _____

Forgive me as I forgive others.

_____

_____

_____

Character building moments in my refining process.

_____

_____

_____

Filter my feelings through the truth of Your Word.

_____

_____

This is the day that the Lord has made......I will rejoice and be glad in it!

My Daily Bread

Date:_____

Everything He gives me to do..............He's already provided a way to be done!

Opportunity Given	Provision Provided
_____	_____
_____	_____
_____	_____
_____	_____

Your will be done. Praises & Prayers

Answered

_____ _____
_____ _____
_____ _____
_____ _____

Forgive me as I forgive others.

_____
_____
_____

Character building moments in my refining process.

_____
_____
_____

Filter my feelings through the truth of Your Word.

_____
_____

This is the day that the Lord has made......I will rejoice and be glad in it!

My Daily Bread

Date:_____

Everything He gives me to do..............He's already provided a way to be done!

Opportunity Given	Provision Provided
_____	_____
_____	_____
_____	_____
_____	_____

Your will be done. Praises & Prayers

Answered

_____ _____
_____ _____
_____ _____
_____ _____

Forgive me as I forgive others.

_____
_____
_____
_____

Character building moments in my refining process.

_____
_____
_____

Filter my feelings through the truth of Your Word.

_____
_____

This is the day that the Lord has made......I will rejoice and be glad in it!

My Daily Bread

Date:_____

Everything He gives me to do..............He's already provided a way to be done!

Opportunity Given	Provision Provided
_____	_____
_____	_____
_____	_____
_____	_____

Your will be done. Praises & Prayers

Answered

Forgive me as I forgive others.

Character building moments in my refining process.

Filter my feelings through the truth of Your Word.

This is the day that the Lord has made......I will rejoice and be glad in it!

My Daily Bread

Date:_____

Everything He gives me to do..............He's already provided a way to be done!

Opportunity Given   Provision Provided

_____   _____

_____   _____

_____   _____

_____   _____

Your will be done. Praises & Prayers

Answered

Forgive me as I forgive others.

Character building moments in my refining process.

Filter my feelings through the truth of Your Word.

This is the day that the Lord has made......I will rejoice and be glad in it!

My Daily Bread

Date:_____

Everything He gives me to do..............He's already provided a way to be done!

Opportunity Given	Provision Provided
_____	_____
_____	_____
_____	_____
_____	_____

Your will be done. Praises & Prayers

Answered

_____   _____
_____   _____
_____   _____
_____   _____

Forgive me as I forgive others.

_____
_____
_____
_____

Character building moments in my refining process.

_____
_____
_____

Filter my feelings through the truth of Your Word.

_____
_____

This is the day that the Lord has made......I will rejoice and be glad in it!

My Daily Bread

Date:_____

Everything He gives me to do..............He's already provided a way to be done!

Opportunity Given	Provision Provided
_____	_____
_____	_____
_____	_____

Your will be done. Praises & Prayers

Answered

_____ _____
_____ _____
_____ _____
_____ _____

Forgive me as I forgive others.

_____
_____
_____

Character building moments in my refining process.

_____
_____
_____

Filter my feelings through the truth of Your Word.

_____
_____

This is the day that the Lord has made......I will rejoice and be glad in it!

My Daily Bread   Date:_____

Everything He gives me to do..............He's already provided a way to be done!

Opportunity Given	Provision Provided
_____	_____
_____	_____
_____	_____
_____	_____

Your will be done. Praises & Prayers

Answered

_____   _____

_____   _____

_____   _____

_____   _____

Forgive me as I forgive others.

Character building moments in my refining process.

Filter my feelings through the truth of Your Word.

This is the day that the Lord has made......I will rejoice and be glad in it!

My Daily Bread

Date:_____

Everything He gives me to do..............He's already provided a way to be done!

Opportunity Given	Provision Provided
_____	_____
_____	_____
_____	_____
_____	_____

Your will be done. Praises & Prayers

Answered

_____ _____
_____ _____
_____ _____
_____ _____

Forgive me as I forgive others.

_____
_____
_____

Character building moments in my refining process.

_____
_____
_____

Filter my feelings through the truth of Your Word.

_____
_____

This is the day that the Lord has made......I will rejoice and be glad in it!

My Daily Bread

Everything He gives me to do..............He's already provided a way to be done!

Opportunity Given   Provision Provided

_____   _____

_____   _____

_____   _____

_____   _____

Your will be done. Praises & Prayers

Answered

_____   _____

_____   _____

_____   _____

_____   _____

Forgive me as I forgive others.

_____

_____

_____

Character building moments in my refining process.

_____

_____

Filter my feelings through the truth of Your Word.

_____

_____

This is the day that the Lord has made......I will rejoice and be glad in it!

My Daily Bread

Date:_____

Everything He gives me to do..............He's already provided a way to be done!

Opportunity Given	Provision Provided

Your will be done. Praises & Prayers

Answered

Forgive me as I forgive others.

Character building moments in my refining process.

Filter my feelings through the truth of Your Word.

This is the day that the Lord has made......I will rejoice and be glad in it!

My Daily Bread

Date:_____

Everything He gives me to do..............He's already provided a way to be done!

Opportunity Given	Provision Provided
_____	_____
_____	_____
_____	_____
_____	_____

Your will be done. Praises & Prayers

Answered

_____ _____
_____ _____
_____ _____
_____ _____

Forgive me as I forgive others.

Character building moments in my refining process.

Filter my feelings through the truth of Your Word.

This is the day that the Lord has made......I will rejoice and be glad in it!

My Daily Bread

Date:_____

Everything He gives me to do..............He's already provided a way to be done!

Opportunity Given   Provision Provided

_____   _____

_____   _____

_____   _____

_____   _____

Your will be done. Praises & Prayers

Answered

_____   _____

_____   _____

_____   _____

_____   _____

Forgive me as I forgive others.

_____

_____

_____

Character building moments in my refining process.

_____

_____

_____

Filter my feelings through the truth of Your Word.

_____

_____

This is the day that the Lord has made......I will rejoice and be glad in it!

My Daily Bread

Date:_____

Everything He gives me to do..............He's already provided a way to be done!

Opportunity Given	Provision Provided
_____	_____
_____	_____
_____	_____
_____	_____

Your will be done. Praises & Prayers

Answered

Forgive me as I forgive others.

Character building moments in my refining process.

Filter my feelings through the truth of Your Word.

This is the day that the Lord has made......I will rejoice and be glad in it!

My Daily Bread

Date:_____

Everything He gives me to do..............He's already provided a way to be done!

Opportunity Given	Provision Provided
_____	_____
_____	_____
_____	_____
_____	_____

Your will be done. Praises & Prayers

Answered

_____ _____

_____ _____

_____ _____

_____ _____

Forgive me as I forgive others.

_____

_____

_____

Character building moments in my refining process.

_____

_____

_____

Filter my feelings through the truth of Your Word.

_____

_____

This is the day that the Lord has made......I will rejoice and be glad in it!

My Daily Bread

Everything He gives me to do..............He's already provided a way to be done!

Opportunity Given	Provision Provided
_____	_____
_____	_____
_____	_____
_____	_____

Your will be done. Praises & Prayers

Answered

_____	_____
_____	_____
_____	_____
_____	_____

Forgive me as I forgive others.

_____

_____

_____

_____

Character building moments in my refining process.

_____

_____

_____

Filter my feelings through the truth of Your Word.

_____

_____

This is the day that the Lord has made......I will rejoice and be glad in it!

My Daily Bread

Date:_____

Everything He gives me to do..............He's already provided a way to be done!

Opportunity Given	Provision Provided
_____	_____
_____	_____
_____	_____
_____	_____

Your will be done. Praises & Prayers

Answered

_____ _____

_____ _____

_____ _____

_____ _____

Forgive me as I forgive others.

_____

_____

_____

Character building moments in my refining process.

_____

_____

_____

Filter my feelings through the truth of Your Word.

_____

_____

This is the day that the Lord has made......I will rejoice and be glad in it!

My Daily Bread

Date:_____

Everything He gives me to do..............He's already provided a way to be done!

Opportunity Given	Provision Provided
_____	_____
_____	_____
_____	_____
_____	_____

Your will be done. Praises & Prayers

Answered

_____ _____

_____ _____

_____ _____

_____ _____

Forgive me as I forgive others.

_____

_____

_____

Character building moments in my refining process.

_____

_____

_____

Filter my feelings through the truth of Your Word.

_____

_____

This is the day that the Lord has made......I will rejoice and be glad in it!

My Daily Bread

Date:_____

Everything He gives me to do..............He's already provided a way to be done!

Opportunity Given	Provision Provided
_____	_____
_____	_____
_____	_____
_____	_____

Your will be done. Praises & Prayers

Answered

Forgive me as I forgive others.

Character building moments in my refining process.

Filter my feelings through the truth of Your Word.

This is the day that the Lord has made......I will rejoice and be glad in it!

My Daily Bread

Everything He gives me to do..............He's already provided a way to be done!

Opportunity Given	Provision Provided
_____	_____
_____	_____
_____	_____
_____	_____

Your will be done. Praises & Prayers

Answered

_____   _____

_____   _____

_____   _____

_____   _____

Forgive me as I forgive others.

_____

_____

_____

Character building moments in my refining process.

_____

_____

_____

Filter my feelings through the truth of Your Word.

_____

_____

This is the day that the Lord has made......I will rejoice and be glad in it!

My Daily Bread

Date:_____

Everything He gives me to do..............He's already provided a way to be done!

Opportunity Given	Provision Provided
_____	_____
_____	_____
_____	_____
_____	_____

Your will be done. Praises & Prayers

Answered

_____ _____

_____ _____

_____ _____

_____ _____

Forgive me as I forgive others.

_____
_____
_____

Character building moments in my refining process.

_____
_____
_____

Filter my feelings through the truth of Your Word.

_____
_____

This is the day that the Lord has made......I will rejoice and be glad in it!

My Daily Bread

Date:_____

Everything He gives me to do..............He's already provided a way to be done!

Opportunity Given	Provision Provided
_____	_____
_____	_____
_____	_____
_____	_____

Your will be done. Praises & Prayers

Answered

_____ _____
_____ _____
_____ _____
_____ _____

Forgive me as I forgive others.

_____
_____
_____

Character building moments in my refining process.

_____
_____
_____

Filter my feelings through the truth of Your Word.

_____
_____

This is the day that the Lord has made......I will rejoice and be glad in it!

My Daily Bread

Date:_____

Everything He gives me to do..............He's already provided a way to be done!

Opportunity Given   Provision Provided

_____   _____

_____   _____

_____   _____

_____   _____

Your will be done. Praises & Prayers

Answered

_____ _____

_____ _____

_____ _____

_____ _____

Forgive me as I forgive others.

_____

_____

_____

Character building moments in my refining process.

_____

_____

_____

Filter my feelings through the truth of Your Word.

_____

_____

This is the day that the Lord has made......I will rejoice and be glad in it!

LOVE

THE GODLY CHARACTER OF LOVE

Love is patient, love is kind. It does not envy, it does not boast, it is not proud. It is not rude, it is not self-seeking, it is not easily angered, it keeps no record of wrongs. Love does not delight in evil but rejoices with the truth. It always protects, always trusts, always hopes, always perseveres. Love never fails. (1 Corinthians 13:4-8)

We've all heard the words, "All you need is love," and that is the plain and simple truth as long as you know *who* love is. That's right, who. The bible tells us that God is love. When you read the verse above, every time the word love is mentioned, it is describing God's character. With that understanding, it makes perfect sense why He is all we'll ever need.

Jesus made it possible for us to truly know what love is and to be able to love others, when He made the ultimate sacrifice by giving His life for ours on the cross. His death and resurrection bridged the gap that sin has caused and made a way for our relationship with God to be restored.

The more we grow in our relationship with God the more we come to understand His unending and unconditional love for us. It's in our personal relationship with Christ that we begin to develop the godly character of love and the fruit of that love begins to be displayed in our lives towards others.

How well are you doing in developing the godly character of love? Insert your name every time love is mentioned in the verse below, then ask yourself if that is true of your character.

_____is patient, _____ is kind. _____ does not envy, _____ does not boast, _____ is not proud. _____ is not rude, _____ is not self-seeking, _____is not easily angered, _____ keeps no record of wrongs. _____ does not delight in evil but rejoices with the truth. _____ always protects, always trusts, always hopes, always perseveres. _____ never fails.

BREAD FOR YOUR JOURNEY
GOD'S WORD CONCERNING LOVE

We love because he first loved us.

1 John 4:19

No one can have greater love than to lay down his life for his friends.

John 15:13

A new command I give you: Love one another. As I have loved you, so you must love one another. By this everyone will know that you are my disciples, if you love one another.

John 13:34-35

I pray that out of his glorious riches he may strengthen you with power through his Spirit in your inner being, so that Christ may dwell in your hearts through faith. And I pray that you, being rooted and established in love, may have power, together with all the Lord's holy people, to grasp how wide and long and high and deep is the love of Christ, and to know this love that surpasses knowledge—that you may be filled to the measure of all the fullness of God.

Ephesians 3: 16-18

You have heard the law that says, 'Love your neighbor' and hate your enemy. But I say, love your enemies! Pray for those who persecute you! In that way, you will be acting as true children of your Father in heaven.

Matthew 5:43-45

For I am convinced that neither death nor life, neither angels nor demons, neither the present nor the future, nor any powers, neither height nor depth, nor anything else in all creation, will be able to separate us from the love of God that is in Christ Jesus our Lord.

Romans 8:38-39

Checkpoints Along The Way

Expectations: What would change in my life if I had more Love?

_____

_____

_____

_____

_____

Memorable Moments: What happened when I put Love into practice?

_____

_____

_____

_____

_____

Reaping A Harvest: How has my life improved because of Love?

_____

_____

_____

_____

_____

My Daily Bread

Date:_____

Everything He gives me to do..............He's already provided a way to be done!

Opportunity Given	Provision Provided
_____	_____
_____	_____
_____	_____
_____	_____

Your will be done. Praises & Prayers

Answered

_____ _____
_____ _____
_____ _____
_____ _____

Forgive me as I forgive others.

_____
_____
_____

Character building moments in my refining process.

_____
_____
_____

Filter my feelings through the truth of Your Word.

_____
_____

This is the day that the Lord has made......I will rejoice and be glad in it!

My Daily Bread

Date:_____

Everything He gives me to do..............He's already provided a way to be done!

Opportunity Given	Provision Provided

Your will be done. Praises & Prayers

Answered

Forgive me as I forgive others.

Character building moments in my refining process.

Filter my feelings through the truth of Your Word.

This is the day that the Lord has made......I will rejoice and be glad in it!

My Daily Bread

Date:_____

Everything He gives me to do..............He's already provided a way to be done!

Opportunity Given	Provision Provided
_____	_____
_____	_____
_____	_____
_____	_____

Your will be done. Praises & Prayers

Answered

_____   _____
_____   _____
_____   _____
_____   _____

Forgive me as I forgive others.

_____
_____
_____
_____

Character building moments in my refining process.

_____
_____
_____

Filter my feelings through the truth of Your Word.

_____
_____

This is the day that the Lord has made......I will rejoice and be glad in it!

My Daily Bread

Date:_____

Everything He gives me to do..............He's already provided a way to be done!

Opportunity Given	Provision Provided
_____	_____
_____	_____
_____	_____
_____	_____

Your will be done. Praises & Prayers

Answered

____ _____

____ _____

____ _____

____ _____

Forgive me as I forgive others.

_____

_____

_____

_____

Character building moments in my refining process.

_____

_____

_____

Filter my feelings through the truth of Your Word.

_____

_____

This is the day that the Lord has made......I will rejoice and be glad in it!

My Daily Bread

Date:_____

Everything He gives me to do..............He's already provided a way to be done!

Opportunity Given	Provision Provided
_____	_____
_____	_____
_____	_____
_____	_____

Your will be done. Praises & Prayers

Answered

Forgive me as I forgive others.

Character building moments in my refining process.

Filter my feelings through the truth of Your Word.

This is the day that the Lord has made......I will rejoice and be glad in it!

My Daily Bread

Date:_____

Everything He gives me to do.............He's already provided a way to be done!

Opportunity Given	Provision Provided
_____	_____
_____	_____
_____	_____
_____	_____

Your will be done. Praises & Prayers

Answered

_____ _____

_____ _____

_____ _____

_____ _____

Forgive me as I forgive others.

_____
_____
_____

Character building moments in my refining process.

_____
_____
_____

Filter my feelings through the truth of Your Word.

_____
_____

This is the day that the Lord has made......I will rejoice and be glad in it!

My Daily Bread

Date:_____

Everything He gives me to do..............He's already provided a way to be done!

Opportunity Given	Provision Provided
_____	_____
_____	_____
_____	_____
_____	_____

Your will be done. Praises & Prayers

Answered
_____ _____
_____ _____
_____ _____
_____ _____

Forgive me as I forgive others.

_____
_____
_____

Character building moments in my refining process.

_____
_____

Filter my feelings through the truth of Your Word.

_____
_____

This is the day that the Lord has made......I will rejoice and be glad in it!

My Daily Bread

Date:_____

Everything He gives me to do..............He's already provided a way to be done!

Opportunity Given	Provision Provided
_____	_____
_____	_____
_____	_____
_____	_____

Your will be done. Praises & Prayers

Answered

_____ _____

_____ _____

_____ _____

_____ _____

Forgive me as I forgive others.

_____
_____
_____

Character building moments in my refining process.

_____
_____
_____

Filter my feelings through the truth of Your Word.

_____
_____

This is the day that the Lord has made.......I will rejoice and be glad in it!

My Daily Bread

Date:_____

Everything He gives me to do...............He's already provided a way to be done!

Opportunity Given	Provision Provided
_____	_____
_____	_____
_____	_____
_____	_____

Your will be done. Praises & Prayers

Answered

_____ _____

_____ _____

_____ _____

_____ _____

Forgive me as I forgive others.

_____
_____
_____

Character building moments in my refining process.

_____
_____
_____

Filter my feelings through the truth of Your Word.

_____
_____

This is the day that the Lord has made......I will rejoice and be glad in it!

My Daily Bread

Date:_____

Everything He gives me to do..............He's already provided a way to be done!

Opportunity Given	Provision Provided
_____	_____
_____	_____
_____	_____
_____	_____

Your will be done. Praises & Prayers

Answered

_____   _____

_____   _____

_____   _____

_____   _____

Forgive me as I forgive others.

_____

_____

_____

Character building moments in my refining process.

_____

_____

_____

Filter my feelings through the truth of Your Word.

_____

_____

This is the day that the Lord has made......I will rejoice and be glad in it!

My Daily Bread

Date:_____

Everything He gives me to do..............He's already provided a way to be done!

Opportunity Given	Provision Provided
_____	_____
_____	_____
_____	_____
_____	_____

Your will be done. Praises & Prayers

Answered

_____ _____

_____ _____

_____ _____

_____ _____

Forgive me as I forgive others.

_____

_____

_____

Character building moments in my refining process.

_____

_____

Filter my feelings through the truth of Your Word.

_____

_____

This is the day that the Lord has made......I will rejoice and be glad in it!

My Daily Bread

Date:_____

Everything He gives me to do..............He's already provided a way to be done!

Opportunity Given   Provision Provided

_____   _____
_____   _____
_____   _____
_____   _____

Your will be done. Praises & Prayers

Answered

_____   _____
_____   _____
_____   _____
_____   _____

Forgive me as I forgive others.

_____
_____
_____

Character building moments in my refining process.

_____
_____
_____

Filter my feelings through the truth of Your Word.

_____
_____

This is the day that the Lord has made......I will rejoice and be glad in it!

My Daily Bread

Date:_____

Everything He gives me to do..............He's already provided a way to be done!

Opportunity Given	Provision Provided
_____	_____
_____	_____
_____	_____
_____	_____

Your will be done. Praises & Prayers

Answered

_____ _____

_____ _____

_____ _____

_____ _____

Forgive me as I forgive others.

_____

_____

_____

Character building moments in my refining process.

_____

_____

_____

Filter my feelings through the truth of Your Word.

_____

_____

This is the day that the Lord has made......I will rejoice and be glad in it!

My Daily Bread

Date:_____

Everything He gives me to do..............He's already provided a way to be done!

Opportunity Given   Provision Provided

_____   _____

_____   _____

_____   _____

_____   _____

Your will be done. Praises & Prayers

Answered

_____ _____

_____ _____

_____ _____

_____ _____

Forgive me as I forgive others.

_____

_____

_____

Character building moments in my refining process.

_____

_____

_____

Filter my feelings through the truth of Your Word.

_____

_____

This is the day that the Lord has made......I will rejoice and be glad in it!

My Daily Bread

Date:_____

Everything He gives me to do…………..He's already provided a way to be done!

Opportunity Given	Provision Provided
_____	_____
_____	_____
_____	_____
_____	_____

Your will be done. Praises & Prayers

Answered

_____	_____
_____	_____
_____	_____
_____	_____

Forgive me as I forgive others.

Character building moments in my refining process.

Filter my feelings through the truth of Your Word.

This is the day that the Lord has made……I will rejoice and be glad in it!

My Daily Bread

Date:_____

Everything He gives me to do..............He's already provided a way to be done!

Opportunity Given	Provision Provided
_____	_____
_____	_____
_____	_____
_____	_____

Your will be done. Praises & Prayers

Answered

_____ _____

_____ _____

_____ _____

_____ _____

Forgive me as I forgive others.

_____

_____

_____

Character building moments in my refining process.

_____

_____

_____

Filter my feelings through the truth of Your Word.

_____

_____

This is the day that the Lord has made......I will rejoice and be glad in it!

My Daily Bread

Date:_____

Everything He gives me to do..............He's already provided a way to be done!

Opportunity Given	Provision Provided
_____	_____
_____	_____
_____	_____
_____	_____

Your will be done. Praises & Prayers

Answered

_____ _____

_____ _____

_____ _____

_____ _____

Forgive me as I forgive others.

_____
_____
_____

Character building moments in my refining process.

_____
_____
_____

Filter my feelings through the truth of Your Word.

_____
_____

This is the day that the Lord has made......I will rejoice and be glad in it!

My Daily Bread

Date:_____

Everything He gives me to do...............He's already provided a way to be done!

Opportunity Given	Provision Provided
_____	_____
_____	_____
_____	_____
_____	_____

Your will be done. Praises & Prayers

Answered

_____ _____

_____ _____

_____ _____

_____ _____

Forgive me as I forgive others.

_____

_____

_____

Character building moments in my refining process.

_____

_____

_____

Filter my feelings through the truth of Your Word.

_____

_____

This is the day that the Lord has made......I will rejoice and be glad in it!

My Daily Bread

Date:_____

Everything He gives me to do..............He's already provided a way to be done!

Opportunity Given	Provision Provided
_____	_____
_____	_____
_____	_____
_____	_____

Your will be done. Praises & Prayers

Answered

_____	_____
_____	_____
_____	_____
_____	_____

Forgive me as I forgive others.

_____
_____
_____

Character building moments in my refining process.

_____
_____
_____

Filter my feelings through the truth of Your Word.

_____
_____

This is the day that the Lord has made......I will rejoice and be glad in it!

My Daily Bread

Date:_____

Everything He gives me to do..............He's already provided a way to be done!

Opportunity Given	Provision Provided
_____	_____
_____	_____
_____	_____
_____	_____

Your will be done. Praises & Prayers

Answered

_____ _____

_____ _____

_____ _____

_____ _____

Forgive me as I forgive others.

Character building moments in my refining process.

Filter my feelings through the truth of Your Word.

This is the day that the Lord has made......I will rejoice and be glad in it!

My Daily Bread

Date:_____

Everything He gives me to do...............He's already provided a way to be done!

Opportunity Given	Provision Provided
_____	_____
_____	_____
_____	_____
_____	_____

Your will be done. Praises & Prayers

Answered

_____ _____

_____ _____

_____ _____

_____ _____

Forgive me as I forgive others.

_____

_____

_____

Character building moments in my refining process.

_____

_____

_____

Filter my feelings through the truth of Your Word.

_____

_____

This is the day that the Lord has made......I will rejoice and be glad in it!

My Daily Bread

Date:_____

Everything He gives me to do..............He's already provided a way to be done!

Opportunity Given   Provision Provided

_____   _____

_____   _____

_____   _____

_____   _____

Your will be done. Praises & Prayers

Answered

_____   _____

_____   _____

_____   _____

_____   _____

Forgive me as I forgive others.

_____

_____

_____

Character building moments in my refining process.

_____

_____

_____

Filter my feelings through the truth of Your Word.

_____

_____

This is the day that the Lord has made......I will rejoice and be glad in it!

My Daily Bread

Date:_____

Everything He gives me to do..............He's already provided a way to be done!

Opportunity Given	Provision Provided
_____	_____
_____	_____
_____	_____
_____	_____

Your will be done. Praises & Prayers

Answered

_____ _____

_____ _____

_____ _____

_____ _____

Forgive me as I forgive others.

_____
_____
_____

Character building moments in my refining process.

_____
_____
_____

Filter my feelings through the truth of Your Word.

_____
_____

This is the day that the Lord has made......I will rejoice and be glad in it!

My Daily Bread

Date:_____

Everything He gives me to do..............He's already provided a way to be done!

Opportunity Given	Provision Provided
_____	_____
_____	_____
_____	_____
_____	_____

Your will be done. Praises & Prayers

Answered
_____
_____
_____
_____

Forgive me as I forgive others.

Character building moments in my refining process.

Filter my feelings through the truth of Your Word.

This is the day that the Lord has made......I will rejoice and be glad in it!

My Daily Bread

Date:_____

Everything He gives me to do..............He's already provided a way to be done!

Opportunity Given	Provision Provided
_____	_____
_____	_____
_____	_____
_____	_____

Your will be done. Praises & Prayers

Answered

_____ _____

_____ _____

_____ _____

_____ _____

Forgive me as I forgive others.

_____
_____
_____
_____

Character building moments in my refining process.

_____
_____
_____

Filter my feelings through the truth of Your Word.

_____
_____

This is the day that the Lord has made......I will rejoice and be glad in it!

My Daily Bread

Date:_____

Everything He gives me to do..............He's already provided a way to be done!

Opportunity Given	Provision Provided
_____	_____
_____	_____
_____	_____
_____	_____

Your will be done. Praises & Prayers

Answered

_____ _____
_____ _____
_____ _____
_____ _____

Forgive me as I forgive others.

_____
_____
_____

Character building moments in my refining process.

_____
_____
_____

Filter my feelings through the truth of Your Word.

_____
_____

This is the day that the Lord has made......I will rejoice and be glad in it!

My Daily Bread

Date:_____

Everything He gives me to do..............He's already provided a way to be done!

Opportunity Given	Provision Provided
_____	_____
_____	_____
_____	_____
_____	_____

Your will be done. Praises & Prayers

Answered

_____ _____

_____ _____

_____ _____

_____ _____

Forgive me as I forgive others.

_____
_____
_____

Character building moments in my refining process.

_____
_____
_____

Filter my feelings through the truth of Your Word.

_____
_____

This is the day that the Lord has made......I will rejoice and be glad in it!

My Daily Bread

Date:_____

Everything He gives me to do..............He's already provided a way to be done!

Opportunity Given	Provision Provided
_____	_____
_____	_____
_____	_____
_____	_____

Your will be done. Praises & Prayers

Answered

_____ _____
_____ _____
_____ _____
_____ _____

Forgive me as I forgive others.

_____
_____
_____

Character building moments in my refining process.

_____
_____
_____

Filter my feelings through the truth of Your Word.

_____
_____

This is the day that the Lord has made......I will rejoice and be glad in it!

My Daily Bread

Date:_____

Everything He gives me to do..............He's already provided a way to be done!

Opportunity Given	Provision Provided
_____	_____
_____	_____
_____	_____
_____	_____

Your will be done. Praises & Prayers

Answered

_____ _____
_____ _____
_____ _____
_____ _____

Forgive me as I forgive others.

_____
_____
_____

Character building moments in my refining process.

_____
_____
_____

Filter my feelings through the truth of Your Word.

_____
_____

This is the day that the Lord has made......I will rejoice and be glad in it!

My Daily Bread

Date:_____

Everything He gives me to do..............He's already provided a way to be done!

Opportunity Given	Provision Provided
_____	_____
_____	_____
_____	_____
_____	_____

Your will be done. Praises & Prayers

Answered

_____ _____

_____ _____

_____ _____

_____ _____

Forgive me as I forgive others.

_____
_____
_____

Character building moments in my refining process.

_____
_____
_____

Filter my feelings through the truth of Your Word.

_____
_____

This is the day that the Lord has made......I will rejoice and be glad in it!

My Daily Bread

Date:_____

Everything He gives me to do..............He's already provided a way to be done!

Opportunity Given	Provision Provided
_____	_____
_____	_____
_____	_____
_____	_____

Your will be done. Praises & Prayers

Answered

_____ _____
_____ _____
_____ _____
_____ _____

Forgive me as I forgive others.

_____
_____
_____

Character building moments in my refining process.

_____
_____
_____

Filter my feelings through the truth of Your Word.

_____
_____

This is the day that the Lord has made......I will rejoice and be glad in it!

Notes

JOY

THE GODLY CHARACTER OF JOY

Though the fig tree does not bud and there are no grapes on the vines,
though the olive crop fails and the fields produce no food, though
there are no sheep in the pen and no cattle in the stalls, yet I
will rejoice in the Lord, I will be joyful in God my Savior.
Habakkuk 3:17-18

Joy is a characteristic in the life of a believer that has the ability to catch the attention of the world. It enables you to meet the challenges of life with enthusiasm and expectancy and flows from a deep conviction that God is alive, real and in control of your life.

The world needs to see joyful believers who can praise the Lord no matter what their circumstances are or what their lot in life may be. It gives them hope for their own circumstances and a curiosity to know more about this incredible God we serve.

Joy is an effective, spiritual gift given by God to believers that helps to sustain us in difficult times and increase our happiness in good times. As believers we always have something to be joyful about. Our lives have been forever changed because of the cross. We have been saved by grace, by a Savior that unconditionally loves us and the joy of our salvation leads us to witness to a lost world that deeply needs Jesus.

Joy is a choice we make to praise God with a grateful heart even when life hurts, knowing that the future holds the promise of eternal life with Christ. The fruit of the Holy Spirit displayed in our lives will not go unnoticed by the people around us and will make an impact in our world. This kind of joy is contagious and brings excitement as we share our faith knowing that the joy of the Lord is our strength.

BREAD FOR YOUR JOURNEY
GOD'S WORD CONCERNING JOY

Consider it pure joy, my brothers and sisters, whenever you face trials of many kinds, because you know that the testing of your faith produces perseverance.

James 1:2-3

I delight greatly in the Lord;
my soul rejoices in my God.
For he has clothed me with garments of salvation
and arrayed me in a robe of his righteousness,
as a bridegroom adorns his head like a priest,
and as a bride adorns herself with her jewels.

Isaiah 61:10

For his anger lasts only a moment, but his favor lasts a lifetime;
weeping may stay for the night, but rejoicing comes in the morning

Psalm 30:5

A cheerful heart is good medicine,
but a crushed spirit dries up the bones.

Proverbs 17:22

Nehemiah said, "Go and enjoy choice food and sweet drinks, and send some to those who have nothing prepared. This day is holy to our Lord. Do not grieve, for the joy of the Lord is your strength."

Nehemiah 8:10

Rejoice always, pray continually, give thanks in all circumstances; for this is God's will for you in Christ Jesus.

1 Thessalonians 5:16-18

Checkpoints Along The Way

Expectations: What would change in my life if I had more Joy?

_____

_____

_____

_____

_____

Memorable Moments: What happened when I put Joy into practice?

_____

_____

_____

_____

_____

Reaping A Harvest: How has my life improved because of Joy?

_____

_____

_____

_____

_____

My Daily Bread

Date:_____

Everything He gives me to do..............He's already provided a way to be done!

Opportunity Given	Provision Provided
_____	_____
_____	_____
_____	_____
_____	_____

Your will be done. Praises & Prayers

Answered

_____ _____
_____ _____
_____ _____
_____ _____

Forgive me as I forgive others.

_____
_____
_____

Character building moments in my refining process.

_____
_____
_____

Filter my feelings through the truth of Your Word.

_____
_____

This is the day that the Lord has made......I will rejoice and be glad in it!

My Daily Bread

Date:_____

Everything He gives me to do..............He's already provided a way to be done!

Opportunity Given	Provision Provided
_____	_____
_____	_____
_____	_____
_____	_____

Your will be done. Praises & Prayers

Answered

_____   _____
_____   _____
_____   _____
_____   _____

Forgive me as I forgive others.

_____
_____
_____

Character building moments in my refining process.

_____
_____
_____

Filter my feelings through the truth of Your Word.

_____
_____

This is the day that the Lord has made......I will rejoice and be glad in it!

My Daily Bread

Date:_____

Everything He gives me to do..............He's already provided a way to be done!

Opportunity Given	Provision Provided
_____	_____
_____	_____
_____	_____
_____	_____

Your will be done. Praises & Prayers

Answered

_____ _____

_____ _____

_____ _____

_____ _____

Forgive me as I forgive others.

_____

_____

_____

Character building moments in my refining process.

_____

_____

_____

Filter my feelings through the truth of Your Word.

_____

_____

This is the day that the Lord has made......I will rejoice and be glad in it!

My Daily Bread

Date:_____

Everything He gives me to do..............He's already provided a way to be done!

Opportunity Given	Provision Provided
_____	_____
_____	_____
_____	_____
_____	_____

Your will be done. Praises & Prayers

Answered

_____ _____

_____ _____

_____ _____

_____ _____

Forgive me as I forgive others.

Character building moments in my refining process.

Filter my feelings through the truth of Your Word.

This is the day that the Lord has made......I will rejoice and be glad in it!

My Daily Bread   Date:_____

Everything He gives me to do..............He's already provided a way to be done!

Opportunity Given	Provision Provided
_____	_____
_____	_____
_____	_____
_____	_____

Your will be done. Praises & Prayers

Answered

_____	_____
_____	_____
_____	_____
_____	_____

Forgive me as I forgive others.

_____
_____
_____

Character building moments in my refining process.

_____
_____
_____

Filter my feelings through the truth of Your Word.

_____
_____

This is the day that the Lord has made......I will rejoice and be glad in it!

My Daily Bread

Date:_____

Everything He gives me to do..............He's already provided a way to be done!

Opportunity Given	Provision Provided
_____	_____
_____	_____
_____	_____
_____	_____

Your will be done. Praises & Prayers

Answered

_____   _____
_____   _____
_____   _____
_____   _____

Forgive me as I forgive others.

_____
_____
_____

Character building moments in my refining process.

_____
_____
_____

Filter my feelings through the truth of Your Word.

_____
_____

This is the day that the Lord has made......I will rejoice and be glad in it!

My Daily Bread

Date:_____

Everything He gives me to do..............He's already provided a way to be done!

Opportunity Given	Provision Provided
_____	_____
_____	_____
_____	_____
_____	_____

Your will be done. Praises & Prayers

Answered

_____ _____
_____ _____
_____ _____
_____ _____

Forgive me as I forgive others.

_____
_____
_____

Character building moments in my refining process.

_____
_____
_____

Filter my feelings through the truth of Your Word.

_____
_____

This is the day that the Lord has made......I will rejoice and be glad in it!

My Daily Bread

Date:_____

Everything He gives me to do..............He's already provided a way to be done!

Opportunity Given	Provision Provided
_____	_____
_____	_____
_____	_____
_____	_____

Your will be done. Praises & Prayers

Answered

_____ _____
_____ _____
_____ _____
_____ _____

Forgive me as I forgive others.

_____
_____
_____

Character building moments in my refining process.

_____
_____
_____

Filter my feelings through the truth of Your Word.

_____
_____

This is the day that the Lord has made......I will rejoice and be glad in it!

My Daily Bread

Date:_____

Everything He gives me to do..............He's already provided a way to be done!

Opportunity Given	Provision Provided

Your will be done. Praises & Prayers

Answered

Forgive me as I forgive others.

Character building moments in my refining process.

Filter my feelings through the truth of Your Word.

This is the day that the Lord has made......I will rejoice and be glad in it!

My Daily Bread

Date:_____

Everything He gives me to do..............He's already provided a way to be done!

Opportunity Given   Provision Provided

Your will be done. Praises & Prayers

Answered

Forgive me as I forgive others.

Character building moments in my refining process.

Filter my feelings through the truth of Your Word.

This is the day that the Lord has made......I will rejoice and be glad in it!

My Daily Bread

Date:_____

Everything He gives me to do..............He's already provided a way to be done!

Opportunity Given	Provision Provided
_____	_____
_____	_____
_____	_____
_____	_____

Your will be done. Praises & Prayers

Answered

_____ _____
_____ _____
_____ _____
_____ _____

Forgive me as I forgive others.

_____
_____
_____

Character building moments in my refining process.

_____
_____
_____

Filter my feelings through the truth of Your Word.

_____
_____

This is the day that the Lord has made......I will rejoice and be glad in it!

My Daily Bread

Date:_____

Everything He gives me to do..............He's already provided a way to be done!

Opportunity Given	Provision Provided
_____	_____
_____	_____
_____	_____
_____	_____

Your will be done. Praises & Prayers

Answered

_____ _____

_____ _____

_____ _____

_____ _____

Forgive me as I forgive others.

_____

_____

_____

Character building moments in my refining process.

_____

_____

_____

Filter my feelings through the truth of Your Word.

_____

_____

This is the day that the Lord has made......I will rejoice and be glad in it!

My Daily Bread

Everything He gives me to do..............He's already provided a way to be done!

Opportunity Given	Provision Provided
_____	_____
_____	_____
_____	_____
_____	_____

Your will be done. Praises & Prayers

Answered

_____ _____

_____ _____

_____ _____

_____ _____

Forgive me as I forgive others.

_____

_____

_____

_____

Character building moments in my refining process.

_____

_____

_____

Filter my feelings through the truth of Your Word.

_____

_____

This is the day that the Lord has made......I will rejoice and be glad in it!

My Daily Bread

Date:_____

Everything He gives me to do..............He's already provided a way to be done!

Opportunity Given	Provision Provided
_____	_____
_____	_____
_____	_____
_____	_____

Your will be done. Praises & Prayers

Answered

_____ _____
_____ _____
_____ _____
_____ _____

Forgive me as I forgive others.

_____
_____
_____

Character building moments in my refining process.

_____
_____
_____

Filter my feelings through the truth of Your Word.

_____
_____

This is the day that the Lord has made......I will rejoice and be glad in it!

My Daily Bread

Date:_____

Everything He gives me to do..............He's already provided a way to be done!

Opportunity Given	Provision Provided
_____	_____
_____	_____
_____	_____
_____	_____

Your will be done. Praises & Prayers

Answered

Forgive me as I forgive others.

Character building moments in my refining process.

Filter my feelings through the truth of Your Word.

This is the day that the Lord has made......I will rejoice and be glad in it!

My Daily Bread

Date:_____

Everything He gives me to do...............He's already provided a way to be done!

Opportunity Given	Provision Provided
_____	_____
_____	_____
_____	_____
_____	_____

Your will be done. Praises & Prayers

Answered

_____ _____

_____ _____

_____ _____

_____ _____

Forgive me as I forgive others.

Character building moments in my refining process.

Filter my feelings through the truth of Your Word.

This is the day that the Lord has made......I will rejoice and be glad in it!

My Daily Bread

Date:_____

Everything He gives me to do..............He's already provided a way to be done!

Opportunity Given	Provision Provided
_____	_____
_____	_____
_____	_____
_____	_____

Your will be done. Praises & Prayers

Answered

_____ _____

_____ _____

_____ _____

_____ _____

Forgive me as I forgive others.

_____

_____

_____

Character building moments in my refining process.

_____

_____

_____

Filter my feelings through the truth of Your Word.

_____

_____

This is the day that the Lord has made......I will rejoice and be glad in it!

My Daily Bread

Date:_____

Everything He gives me to do..............He's already provided a way to be done!

Opportunity Given   Provision Provided

_____   _____

_____   _____

_____   _____

_____   _____

Your will be done. Praises & Prayers

Answered

_____   _____

_____   _____

_____   _____

_____   _____

Forgive me as I forgive others.

_____

_____

_____

Character building moments in my refining process.

_____

_____

_____

Filter my feelings through the truth of Your Word.

_____

_____

This is the day that the Lord has made......I will rejoice and be glad in it!

My Daily Bread

Date:_____

Everything He gives me to do..............He's already provided a way to be done!

Opportunity Given	Provision Provided
_____	_____
_____	_____
_____	_____
_____	_____

Your will be done. Praises & Prayers

Answered

_____ _____
_____ _____
_____ _____
_____ _____

Forgive me as I forgive others.

_____
_____
_____

Character building moments in my refining process.

_____
_____
_____

Filter my feelings through the truth of Your Word.

_____
_____

This is the day that the Lord has made......I will rejoice and be glad in it!

My Daily Bread

Date:_____

Everything He gives me to do..............He's already provided a way to be done!

Opportunity Given	Provision Provided

Your will be done. Praises & Prayers

Answered

Forgive me as I forgive others.

Character building moments in my refining process.

Filter my feelings through the truth of Your Word.

This is the day that the Lord has made......I will rejoice and be glad in it!

My Daily Bread   Date:_____

Everything He gives me to do..............He's already provided a way to be done!

Opportunity Given	Provision Provided
_____	_____
_____	_____
_____	_____
_____	_____

Your will be done. Praises & Prayers

Answered

_____ _____
_____ _____
_____ _____
_____ _____

Forgive me as I forgive others.

_____
_____
_____

Character building moments in my refining process.

_____
_____
_____

Filter my feelings through the truth of Your Word.

_____
_____

This is the day that the Lord has made......I will rejoice and be glad in it!

My Daily Bread

Date:_____

Everything He gives me to do..............He's already provided a way to be done!

Opportunity Given	Provision Provided

Your will be done. Praises & Prayers

Answered

Forgive me as I forgive others.

Character building moments in my refining process.

Filter my feelings through the truth of Your Word.

This is the day that the Lord has made......I will rejoice and be glad in it!

My Daily Bread

Date:_____

Everything He gives me to do..............He's already provided a way to be done!

Opportunity Given	Provision Provided
_____	_____
_____	_____
_____	_____
_____	_____

Your will be done. Praises & Prayers

Answered

_____ _____

_____ _____

_____ _____

_____ _____

Forgive me as I forgive others.

_____

_____

_____

Character building moments in my refining process.

_____

_____

_____

Filter my feelings through the truth of Your Word.

_____

_____

This is the day that the Lord has made......I will rejoice and be glad in it!

My Daily Bread

Date:_____

Everything He gives me to do..............He's already provided a way to be done!

Opportunity Given	Provision Provided
_____	_____
_____	_____
_____	_____
_____	_____

Your will be done. Praises & Prayers

Answered

_____ _____

_____ _____

_____ _____

_____ _____

Forgive me as I forgive others.

Character building moments in my refining process.

Filter my feelings through the truth of Your Word.

This is the day that the Lord has made......I will rejoice and be glad in it!

My Daily Bread

Date:_____

Everything He gives me to do..............He's already provided a way to be done!

Opportunity Given	Provision Provided
_____	_____
_____	_____
_____	_____
_____	_____

Your will be done. Praises & Prayers

Answered

_____	_____
_____	_____
_____	_____
_____	_____

Forgive me as I forgive others.

_____
_____
_____
_____

Character building moments in my refining process.

_____
_____
_____

Filter my feelings through the truth of Your Word.

_____
_____

This is the day that the Lord has made......I will rejoice and be glad in it!

My Daily Bread

Date:_____

Everything He gives me to do..............He's already provided a way to be done!

Opportunity Given	Provision Provided
_____	_____
_____	_____
_____	_____
_____	_____

Your will be done. Praises & Prayers

Answered

_____ _____

_____ _____

_____ _____

_____ _____

Forgive me as I forgive others.

_____
_____
_____

Character building moments in my refining process.

_____
_____
_____

Filter my feelings through the truth of Your Word.

_____
_____

This is the day that the Lord has made......I will rejoice and be glad in it!

My Daily Bread

Date:_____

Everything He gives me to do..............He's already provided a way to be done!

Opportunity Given	Provision Provided
_____	_____
_____	_____
_____	_____
_____	_____

Your will be done. Praises & Prayers

Answered

_____	_____
_____	_____
_____	_____
_____	_____

Forgive me as I forgive others.

_____
_____
_____

Character building moments in my refining process.

_____
_____
_____

Filter my feelings through the truth of Your Word.

_____
_____

This is the day that the Lord has made......I will rejoice and be glad in it!

My Daily Bread

Date:_____

Everything He gives me to do..............He's already provided a way to be done!

Opportunity Given	Provision Provided
_____	_____
_____	_____
_____	_____
_____	_____

Your will be done. Praises & Prayers

Answered

_____ _____
_____ _____
_____ _____
_____ _____

Forgive me as I forgive others.

_____
_____
_____

Character building moments in my refining process.

_____
_____
_____

Filter my feelings through the truth of Your Word.

_____
_____

This is the day that the Lord has made......I will rejoice and be glad in it!

My Daily Bread

Everything He gives me to do..............He's already provided a way to be done!

Opportunity Given	Provision Provided

Your will be done. Praises & Prayers

Answered

Forgive me as I forgive others.

Character building moments in my refining process.

Filter my feelings through the truth of Your Word.

This is the day that the Lord has made......I will rejoice and be glad in it!

My Daily Bread

Date:_____

Everything He gives me to do..............He's already provided a way to be done!

Opportunity Given	Provision Provided
_____	_____
_____	_____
_____	_____
_____	_____

Your will be done. Praises & Prayers

Answered

Forgive me as I forgive others.

Character building moments in my refining process.

Filter my feelings through the truth of Your Word.

This is the day that the Lord has made......I will rejoice and be glad in it!

My Daily Bread

Date:_____

Everything He gives me to do..............He's already provided a way to be done!

Opportunity Given	Provision Provided
_____	_____
_____	_____
_____	_____
_____	_____

Your will be done. Praises & Prayers

Answered

_____ _____

_____ _____

_____ _____

_____ _____

Forgive me as I forgive others.

_____

_____

_____

Character building moments in my refining process.

_____

_____

_____

Filter my feelings through the truth of Your Word.

_____

_____

This is the day that the Lord has made......I will rejoice and be glad in it!

Notes

PEACE

THE GODLY CHARACTER OF PEACE

You will guard him and keep him in perfect and constant
peace whose mind is stayed on You, because he commits him-
self to You, leans on You, and hopes confidently in You.

Isaiah 26:3

As each new day begins, news and updates from social media inform us of all the current events taking place in this world. It's easy to become overwhelmed and discouraged at what we see and hear. Jesus told us that we would live in a world with trouble, but He also told us to take heart, be encouraged, because He has overcome the world. Knowing this gives us peace.

That deep spiritual inner peace is ours through Christ regardless of the suffering and distress the world brings. It is found in a personal relationship with Jesus and can be experienced every time we choose to remain focused on the truth and promises of God.

God's Word instructs us to pray when we feel anxious and afraid. Our prayers and petitions take us to the throne of grace, where our Savior, who is able to guard our hearts and minds, reminds us of His truth and replaces our fear with His peace.

We often make the assumption that peace is the absence of chaos and that is not true. Peace is the presence of calm in the midst of chaos. This is the type of peace God is offering and the beautiful thing about the peace of God is that it flows from within your heart. God's peace not only affects how you look and feel about a situation, it impacts how you react to it.

As we develop the Godly character of Peace we discover that Jesus is our refuge, our safe place, the calm in our storms; our Prince of Peace. Knowing that Christ is our peace, allows us to entrust our lives to Him, surrender our burdens, our anxieties, doubts, fears, and restlessness and exchange them for the peace that gives us a confident hope for the future.

BREAD FOR YOUR JOURNEY
GOD'S WORD CONCERNING PEACE

"Do not be anxious about anything, but in every situation, by prayer and petition, with thanksgiving, present your requests to God. And the peace of God, which transcends all understanding, will guard your hearts and your minds in Christ Jesus."

Philippians 4:6-7

*I will lie down and sleep in peace, for you alone,
O Lord, make me dwell in safety.*

Psalm 4:8

Peace I leave with you; my peace I give you. I do not give to you as the world gives. Do not let your hearts be troubled and do not be afraid.

John 14:27

I have told you these things, so that in me you may have peace. In this world you will have trouble. But take heart! I have overcome the world.

John 16:33

Blessed are the peacemakers, for they will be called children of God.

Matthew 5:9

Come to me, all you who are weary and burdened, and I will give you rest. Take my yoke upon you and learn from me, for I am gentle and humble in heart, and you will find rest for your souls. For my yoke is easy and my burden is light.

Matthew 11:28-30

*Those who live in the shelter of the Most High will find rest in the shadow of the Almighty. This I declare about the Lord:
He alone is my refuge, my place of safety; he is my God, and I trust him.*

Psalm 91:1-2

Checkpoints Along The Way

Expectations: What would change in my life if I had more Peace?

_____

_____

_____

_____

_____

Memorable Moments: What happened when I put Peace into practice?

_____

_____

_____

_____

Reaping A Harvest: How has my life improved because of Peace?

_____

_____

_____

_____

My Daily Bread

Date:_____

Everything He gives me to do..............He's already provided a way to be done!

Opportunity Given	Provision Provided
_____	_____
_____	_____
_____	_____
_____	_____

Your will be done. Praises & Prayers

Answered

Forgive me as I forgive others.

Character building moments in my refining process.

Filter my feelings through the truth of Your Word.

This is the day that the Lord has made......I will rejoice and be glad in it!

My Daily Bread

Date:_____

Everything He gives me to do..............He's already provided a way to be done!

Opportunity Given	Provision Provided
_____	_____
_____	_____
_____	_____
_____	_____

Your will be done. Praises & Prayers

Answered

_____ _____

_____ _____

_____ _____

_____ _____

Forgive me as I forgive others.

_____

_____

_____

Character building moments in my refining process.

_____

_____

_____

Filter my feelings through the truth of Your Word.

_____

_____

This is the day that the Lord has made......I will rejoice and be glad in it!

My Daily Bread

Date:_____

Everything He gives me to do..............He's already provided a way to be done!

Opportunity Given	Provision Provided
_____	_____
_____	_____
_____	_____
_____	_____

Your will be done. Praises & Prayers

Answered

_____ _____
_____ _____
_____ _____
_____ _____

Forgive me as I forgive others.

_____
_____
_____

Character building moments in my refining process.

_____
_____
_____

Filter my feelings through the truth of Your Word.

_____
_____

This is the day that the Lord has made......I will rejoice and be glad in it!

My Daily Bread

Date:_____

Everything He gives me to do..............He's already provided a way to be done!

Opportunity Given	Provision Provided
_____	_____
_____	_____
_____	_____
_____	_____

Your will be done. Praises & Prayers

Answered

_____   _____

_____   _____

_____   _____

_____   _____

Forgive me as I forgive others.

_____

_____

_____

Character building moments in my refining process.

_____

_____

_____

Filter my feelings through the truth of Your Word.

_____

_____

This is the day that the Lord has made......I will rejoice and be glad in it!

My Daily Bread

Date:_____

Everything He gives me to do..............He's already provided a way to be done!

Opportunity Given	Provision Provided
_____	_____
_____	_____
_____	_____
_____	_____

Your will be done. Praises & Prayers

Answered

_____ _____

_____ _____

_____ _____

_____ _____

Forgive me as I forgive others.

_____

_____

_____

Character building moments in my refining process.

_____

_____

_____

Filter my feelings through the truth of Your Word.

_____

_____

This is the day that the Lord has made......I will rejoice and be glad in it!

My Daily Bread

Date:_____

Everything He gives me to do..............He's already provided a way to be done!

Opportunity Given	Provision Provided
_____	_____
_____	_____
_____	_____
_____	_____

Your will be done. Praises & Prayers

Answered
_____ _____
_____ _____
_____ _____
_____ _____

Forgive me as I forgive others.

_____
_____
_____

Character building moments in my refining process.

_____
_____
_____

Filter my feelings through the truth of Your Word.

_____
_____

This is the day that the Lord has made......I will rejoice and be glad in it!

My Daily Bread

Date:_____

Everything He gives me to do..............He's already provided a way to be done!

Opportunity Given	Provision Provided
_____	_____
_____	_____
_____	_____
_____	_____

Your will be done. Praises & Prayers

Answered

_____ _____

_____ _____

_____ _____

_____ _____

Forgive me as I forgive others.

_____

_____

_____

Character building moments in my refining process.

_____

_____

_____

Filter my feelings through the truth of Your Word.

_____

_____

This is the day that the Lord has made......I will rejoice and be glad in it!

My Daily Bread

Date:_____

Everything He gives me to do..............He's already provided a way to be done!

Opportunity Given	Provision Provided

Your will be done. Praises & Prayers

Answered

Forgive me as I forgive others.

Character building moments in my refining process.

Filter my feelings through the truth of Your Word.

This is the day that the Lord has made......I will rejoice and be glad in it!

My Daily Bread

Date:_____

Everything He gives me to do..............He's already provided a way to be done!

Opportunity Given	Provision Provided
_____	_____
_____	_____
_____	_____
_____	_____

Your will be done. Praises & Prayers

Answered

Forgive me as I forgive others.

Character building moments in my refining process.

Filter my feelings through the truth of Your Word.

This is the day that the Lord has made......I will rejoice and be glad in it!

My Daily Bread

Date:_____

Everything He gives me to do..............He's already provided a way to be done!

Opportunity Given	Provision Provided
_____	_____
_____	_____
_____	_____
_____	_____

Your will be done. Praises & Prayers

Answered

Forgive me as I forgive others.

Character building moments in my refining process.

Filter my feelings through the truth of Your Word.

This is the day that the Lord has made......I will rejoice and be glad in it!

My Daily Bread

Date:_____

Everything He gives me to do..............He's already provided a way to be done!

Opportunity Given	Provision Provided
_____	_____
_____	_____
_____	_____
_____	_____

Your will be done. Praises & Prayers

Answered

_____ _____

_____ _____

_____ _____

_____ _____

Forgive me as I forgive others.

_____
_____
_____

Character building moments in my refining process.

_____
_____
_____

Filter my feelings through the truth of Your Word.

_____
_____

This is the day that the Lord has made......I will rejoice and be glad in it!

My Daily Bread

Date:_____

Everything He gives me to do..............He's already provided a way to be done!

Opportunity Given	Provision Provided
_____	_____
_____	_____
_____	_____
_____	_____

Your will be done. Praises & Prayers

Answered

_____ _____

_____ _____

_____ _____

_____ _____

Forgive me as I forgive others.

_____

_____

_____

_____

Character building moments in my refining process.

_____

_____

_____

Filter my feelings through the truth of Your Word.

_____

_____

This is the day that the Lord has made......I will rejoice and be glad in it!

My Daily Bread

Date:_____

Everything He gives me to do..............He's already provided a way to be done!

Opportunity Given	Provision Provided
_____	_____
_____	_____
_____	_____
_____	_____

Your will be done. Praises & Prayers

Answered

_____ _____

_____ _____

_____ _____

_____ _____

Forgive me as I forgive others.

_____

_____

_____

Character building moments in my refining process.

_____

_____

_____

Filter my feelings through the truth of Your Word.

_____

_____

This is the day that the Lord has made......I will rejoice and be glad in it!

My Daily Bread

Date:_____

Everything He gives me to do..............He's already provided a way to be done!

Opportunity Given	Provision Provided

Your will be done. Praises & Prayers

Answered

Forgive me as I forgive others.

Character building moments in my refining process.

Filter my feelings through the truth of Your Word.

This is the day that the Lord has made......I will rejoice and be glad in it!

My Daily Bread

Date:_____

Everything He gives me to do.............He's already provided a way to be done!

Opportunity Given	Provision Provided
_____	_____
_____	_____
_____	_____
_____	_____

Your will be done. Praises & Prayers

Answered

_____   _____

_____   _____

_____   _____

_____   _____

Forgive me as I forgive others.

_____

_____

_____

Character building moments in my refining process.

_____

_____

_____

Filter my feelings through the truth of Your Word.

_____

_____

This is the day that the Lord has made......I will rejoice and be glad in it!

My Daily Bread

Date:_____

Everything He gives me to do..............He's already provided a way to be done!

Opportunity Given	Provision Provided
_____	_____
_____	_____
_____	_____
_____	_____

Your will be done. Praises & Prayers

Answered

_____	_____
_____	_____
_____	_____
_____	_____

Forgive me as I forgive others.

Character building moments in my refining process.

Filter my feelings through the truth of Your Word.

This is the day that the Lord has made......I will rejoice and be glad in it!

My Daily Bread

Date:_____

Everything He gives me to do..............He's already provided a way to be done!

Opportunity Given	Provision Provided
_____	_____
_____	_____
_____	_____
_____	_____

Your will be done. Praises & Prayers

Answered

_____ _____
_____ _____
_____ _____
_____ _____

Forgive me as I forgive others.

_____
_____
_____

Character building moments in my refining process.

_____
_____
_____

Filter my feelings through the truth of Your Word.

_____
_____

This is the day that the Lord has made......I will rejoice and be glad in it!

My Daily Bread

Date:_____

Everything He gives me to do..............He's already provided a way to be done!

Opportunity Given	Provision Provided
_____	_____
_____	_____
_____	_____
_____	_____

Your will be done. Praises & Prayers

Answered

Forgive me as I forgive others.

Character building moments in my refining process.

Filter my feelings through the truth of Your Word.

This is the day that the Lord has made......I will rejoice and be glad in it!

My Daily Bread

Date:_____

Everything He gives me to do..............He's already provided a way to be done!

Opportunity Given	Provision Provided
_____	_____
_____	_____
_____	_____
_____	_____

Your will be done. Praises & Prayers

Answered

_____ _____

_____ _____

_____ _____

_____ _____

Forgive me as I forgive others.

_____

_____

_____

Character building moments in my refining process.

_____

_____

_____

Filter my feelings through the truth of Your Word.

_____

_____

This is the day that the Lord has made......I will rejoice and be glad in it!

My Daily Bread

Date:_____

Everything He gives me to do..............He's already provided a way to be done!

Opportunity Given	Provision Provided
_____	_____
_____	_____
_____	_____
_____	_____

Your will be done. Praises & Prayers

Answered

_____ _____

_____ _____

_____ _____

_____ _____

Forgive me as I forgive others.

_____

_____

_____

Character building moments in my refining process.

_____

_____

_____

Filter my feelings through the truth of Your Word.

_____

_____

This is the day that the Lord has made......I will rejoice and be glad in it!

My Daily Bread

Date:_____

Everything He gives me to do...............He's already provided a way to be done!

Opportunity Given	Provision Provided

Your will be done. Praises & Prayers

Answered

Forgive me as I forgive others.

Character building moments in my refining process.

Filter my feelings through the truth of Your Word.

This is the day that the Lord has made......I will rejoice and be glad in it!

My Daily Bread

Date:_____

Everything He gives me to do..............He's already provided a way to be done!

Opportunity Given	Provision Provided
_____	_____
_____	_____
_____	_____
_____	_____

Your will be done. Praises & Prayers

Answered

_____ _____

_____ _____

_____ _____

_____ _____

Forgive me as I forgive others.

_____

_____

_____

Character building moments in my refining process.

_____

_____

_____

Filter my feelings through the truth of Your Word.

_____

_____

This is the day that the Lord has made......I will rejoice and be glad in it!

My Daily Bread

Date:_____

Everything He gives me to do..............He's already provided a way to be done!

Opportunity Given	Provision Provided
_____	_____
_____	_____
_____	_____
_____	_____

Your will be done. Praises & Prayers

Answered

_____ _____

_____ _____

_____ _____

_____ _____

Forgive me as I forgive others.

_____

_____

_____

Character building moments in my refining process.

_____

_____

_____

Filter my feelings through the truth of Your Word.

_____

_____

This is the day that the Lord has made......I will rejoice and be glad in it!

My Daily Bread

Date:_____

Everything He gives me to do..............He's already provided a way to be done!

Opportunity Given	Provision Provided
_____	_____
_____	_____
_____	_____
_____	_____

Your will be done. Praises & Prayers

Answered

_____   _____

_____   _____

_____   _____

_____   _____

Forgive me as I forgive others.

_____

_____

_____

Character building moments in my refining process.

_____

_____

_____

Filter my feelings through the truth of Your Word.

_____

_____

This is the day that the Lord has made......I will rejoice and be glad in it!

My Daily Bread

Date:_____

Everything He gives me to do...............He's already provided a way to be done!

Opportunity Given	Provision Provided
_____	_____
_____	_____
_____	_____
_____	_____

Your will be done. Praises & Prayers

Answered

_____	_____
_____	_____
_____	_____
_____	_____

Forgive me as I forgive others.

_____
_____
_____

Character building moments in my refining process.

_____
_____

Filter my feelings through the truth of Your Word.

_____
_____

This is the day that the Lord has made......I will rejoice and be glad in it!

My Daily Bread

Everything He gives me to do..............He's already provided a way to be done!

Opportunity Given	Provision Provided
_____	_____
_____	_____
_____	_____
_____	_____

Your will be done. Praises & Prayers

Answered

_____ _____

_____ _____

_____ _____

_____ _____

Forgive me as I forgive others.

_____

_____

_____

Character building moments in my refining process.

_____

_____

_____

Filter my feelings through the truth of Your Word.

_____

_____

This is the day that the Lord has made......I will rejoice and be glad in it!

My Daily Bread

Date:_____

Everything He gives me to do..............He's already provided a way to be done!

Opportunity Given	Provision Provided
_____	_____
_____	_____
_____	_____
_____	_____

Your will be done. Praises & Prayers

Answered

_____ _____

_____ _____

_____ _____

_____ _____

Forgive me as I forgive others.

_____
_____
_____

Character building moments in my refining process.

_____
_____

Filter my feelings through the truth of Your Word.

_____
_____

This is the day that the Lord has made......I will rejoice and be glad in it!

My Daily Bread

Date:_____

Everything He gives me to do..............He's already provided a way to be done!

Opportunity Given	Provision Provided

Your will be done. Praises & Prayers

Answered

Forgive me as I forgive others.

Character building moments in my refining process.

Filter my feelings through the truth of Your Word.

This is the day that the Lord has made......I will rejoice and be glad in it!

My Daily Bread

Date:_____

Everything He gives me to do..............He's already provided a way to be done!

Opportunity Given	Provision Provided
_____	_____
_____	_____
_____	_____
_____	_____

Your will be done. Praises & Prayers

Answered

_____ _____

_____ _____

_____ _____

_____ _____

Forgive me as I forgive others.

_____

_____

_____

_____

Character building moments in my refining process.

_____

_____

_____

Filter my feelings through the truth of Your Word.

_____

_____

This is the day that the Lord has made......I will rejoice and be glad in it!

My Daily Bread

Date:_____

Everything He gives me to do..............He's already provided a way to be done!

Opportunity Given	Provision Provided
_____	_____
_____	_____
_____	_____
_____	_____

Your will be done. Praises & Prayers

Answered

_____ _____

_____ _____

_____ _____

_____ _____

Forgive me as I forgive others.

_____

_____

_____

Character building moments in my refining process.

_____

_____

_____

Filter my feelings through the truth of Your Word.

_____

_____

This is the day that the Lord has made......I will rejoice and be glad in it!

My Daily Bread

Date:_____

Everything He gives me to do...............He's already provided a way to be done!

Opportunity Given	Provision Provided
_____	_____
_____	_____
_____	_____
_____	_____

Your will be done. Praises & Prayers

Answered

____ _____
____ _____
____ _____
____ _____

Forgive me as I forgive others.

_____
_____
_____
_____

Character building moments in my refining process.

_____
_____
_____

Filter my feelings through the truth of Your Word.

_____
_____

This is the day that the Lord has made......I will rejoice and be glad in it!

Notes

PATIENCE

THE GODLY CHARACTER OF PATIENCE

I waited patiently for the Lord; he turned to me and heard my cry. He lifted me out of the slimy pit, out of the mud and the mire; He set my feet on a rock and gave me a firm place to stand. He put a new song in my mouth, a hymn of praise to our God. Many will see and fear the Lord and put their trust in Him.

Psalm 40:1-3

Waiting is difficult and it seems that every day we are faced with situations that require patience. It is a fruit of the Spirit that reminds us how they are all intertwined and blended together to refine our character.

When you are waiting for answers, in traffic, for a slow internet connection or anything else that requires patience, does your attitude reflect the fruit of the Spirit? Are you displaying love, joy, peace, patience, kindness, goodness, faithfulness, gentleness and self -control?

In the parable of the ten virgins, the wise girls were the ones whose lamps were full. They were prepared to withstand the waiting because they had taken the time to store up what would be needed. The moments that require us to exercise patience are opportunities from God to store up the character that is needed as we wait for His Glorious return.

In the waiting the Lord hears our cries and lifts us out of the slimy pit of impatience. He gives us the opportunity to stand on gifts of the Spirit which will change our tune from one of complaining to one of praising.

Our Godly response opens the door to witness to others who will see in us the difference that knowing and following Jesus can make in the lives of those who believe in Him.

Patience is a virtue that is displayed in the life of a Daughter of The King.

BREAD FOR YOUR JOURNEY
GOD'S WORD CONCERNING PATIENCE

Be devoted to one another in love. Honor one another above yourselves. Never be lacking in zeal, but keep your spiritual fervor, serving the Lord. Be joyful in hope, patient in affliction, faithful in prayer.

Romans 12: 10-12

Always be humble, gentle and patient, bearing with one another in love.

Ephesians 4:2

Let us not become weary in doing good, for at the proper time we will reap a harvest if we do not give up.

Galatians 6:9

Wait for the Lord; be strong and take heart and wait for the Lord.

Psalm 27:14

The Lord will fight for you; you need only to be still.

Exodus 14:14

Preach the word; be prepared in season and out of season; correct, rebuke and encourage—with great patience and careful instruction.

2 Timothy 4:2

A hot-tempered person stirs up conflict,

but the one who is patient calms a quarrel.

Proverbs 15:18

But those that wait upon the Lord shall renew their strength; they shall mount up with wings as eagles; they shall run, and not be weary; and they shall walk, and not faint.

Isaiah 40:31

Checkpoints Along The Way

Expectations: What would change in my life if I had more Patience?

_____

_____

_____

_____

_____

Memorable Moments: What happened when I put Patience into practice?

_____

_____

_____

_____

_____

Reaping A Harvest: How has my life improved because of Patience?

_____

_____

_____

_____

_____

My Daily Bread

Date:_____

Everything He gives me to do...............He's already provided a way to be done!

Opportunity Given	Provision Provided
_____	_____
_____	_____
_____	_____
_____	_____

Your will be done. Praises & Prayers

Answered

_____ _____

_____ _____

_____ _____

_____ _____

Forgive me as I forgive others.

_____
_____
_____

Character building moments in my refining process.

_____
_____
_____

Filter my feelings through the truth of Your Word.

_____
_____

This is the day that the Lord has made......I will rejoice and be glad in it!

My Daily Bread

Date:_____

Everything He gives me to do..............He's already provided a way to be done!

Opportunity Given	Provision Provided
_____	_____
_____	_____
_____	_____
_____	_____

Your will be done. Praises & Prayers

Answered

_____   _____

_____   _____

_____   _____

_____   _____

Forgive me as I forgive others.

_____

_____

_____

Character building moments in my refining process.

_____

_____

_____

Filter my feelings through the truth of Your Word.

_____

_____

This is the day that the Lord has made......I will rejoice and be glad in it!

My Daily Bread

Date:_____

Everything He gives me to do..............He's already provided a way to be done!

Opportunity Given	Provision Provided
_____	_____
_____	_____
_____	_____
_____	_____

Your will be done. Praises & Prayers

Answered

_____	_____
_____	_____
_____	_____
_____	_____

Forgive me as I forgive others.

_____
_____
_____

Character building moments in my refining process.

_____
_____
_____

Filter my feelings through the truth of Your Word.

_____
_____

This is the day that the Lord has made......I will rejoice and be glad in it!

My Daily Bread

Date:_____

Everything He gives me to do..............He's already provided a way to be done!

Opportunity Given	Provision Provided
_____	_____
_____	_____
_____	_____
_____	_____

Your will be done. Praises & Prayers

Answered

_____ _____

_____ _____

_____ _____

_____ _____

Forgive me as I forgive others.

_____

_____

_____

Character building moments in my refining process.

_____

_____

_____

Filter my feelings through the truth of Your Word.

_____

_____

This is the day that the Lord has made......I will rejoice and be glad in it!

My Daily Bread

Date:_____

Everything He gives me to do..............He's already provided a way to be done!

Opportunity Given	Provision Provided
_____	_____
_____	_____
_____	_____
_____	_____

Your will be done. Praises & Prayers

Answered

_____ _____

_____ _____

_____ _____

_____ _____

Forgive me as I forgive others.

_____
_____
_____

Character building moments in my refining process.

_____
_____
_____

Filter my feelings through the truth of Your Word.

_____
_____

This is the day that the Lord has made......I will rejoice and be glad in it!

My Daily Bread

Date:_____

Everything He gives me to do..............He's already provided a way to be done!

Opportunity Given	Provision Provided
_____	_____
_____	_____
_____	_____
_____	_____

Your will be done. Praises & Prayers

Answered

_____ _____
_____ _____
_____ _____
_____ _____

Forgive me as I forgive others.

_____
_____
_____

Character building moments in my refining process.

_____
_____
_____

Filter my feelings through the truth of Your Word.

_____
_____

This is the day that the Lord has made......I will rejoice and be glad in it!

My Daily Bread

Date:_____

Everything He gives me to do..............He's already provided a way to be done!

Opportunity Given	Provision Provided
_____	_____
_____	_____
_____	_____
_____	_____

Your will be done. Praises & Prayers

Answered

_____   _____
_____   _____
_____   _____
_____   _____

Forgive me as I forgive others.

_____
_____
_____

Character building moments in my refining process.

_____
_____
_____

Filter my feelings through the truth of Your Word.

_____
_____

This is the day that the Lord has made......I will rejoice and be glad in it!

My Daily Bread

Date:_____

Everything He gives me to do..............He's already provided a way to be done!

Opportunity Given	Provision Provided
_____	_____
_____	_____
_____	_____
_____	_____

Your will be done. Praises & Prayers

Answered

_____ _____
_____ _____
_____ _____
_____ _____

Forgive me as I forgive others.

_____
_____
_____

Character building moments in my refining process.

_____
_____
_____

Filter my feelings through the truth of Your Word.

_____
_____

This is the day that the Lord has made......I will rejoice and be glad in it!

My Daily Bread

Date:_____

Everything He gives me to do..............He's already provided a way to be done!

Opportunity Given	Provision Provided
_____	_____
_____	_____
_____	_____
_____	_____

Your will be done. Praises & Prayers

Answered

Forgive me as I forgive others.

Character building moments in my refining process.

Filter my feelings through the truth of Your Word.

This is the day that the Lord has made......I will rejoice and be glad in it!

My Daily Bread

Date:_____

Everything He gives me to do..............He's already provided a way to be done!

Opportunity Given	Provision Provided
_____	_____
_____	_____
_____	_____
_____	_____

Your will be done. Praises & Prayers

Answered

Forgive me as I forgive others.

Character building moments in my refining process.

Filter my feelings through the truth of Your Word.

This is the day that the Lord has made......I will rejoice and be glad in it!

My Daily Bread

Date:_____

Everything He gives me to do..............He's already provided a way to be done!

Opportunity Given	Provision Provided
_____	_____
_____	_____
_____	_____
_____	_____

Your will be done. Praises & Prayers

Answered

_____ _____

_____ _____

_____ _____

_____ _____

Forgive me as I forgive others.

_____

_____

_____

Character building moments in my refining process.

_____

_____

_____

Filter my feelings through the truth of Your Word.

_____

_____

This is the day that the Lord has made......I will rejoice and be glad in it!

My Daily Bread

Date:_____

Everything He gives me to do..............He's already provided a way to be done!

Opportunity Given	Provision Provided
_____	_____
_____	_____
_____	_____

Your will be done. Praises & Prayers

Answered

_____ _____
_____ _____
_____ _____
_____ _____

Forgive me as I forgive others.

_____
_____
_____

Character building moments in my refining process.

_____
_____
_____

Filter my feelings through the truth of Your Word.

_____
_____

This is the day that the Lord has made......I will rejoice and be glad in it!

My Daily Bread

Date:_____

Everything He gives me to do..............He's already provided a way to be done!

Opportunity Given	Provision Provided
_____	_____
_____	_____
_____	_____
_____	_____

Your will be done. Praises & Prayers

Answered

_____ _____

_____ _____

_____ _____

_____ _____

Forgive me as I forgive others.

Character building moments in my refining process.

Filter my feelings through the truth of Your Word.

This is the day that the Lord has made......I will rejoice and be glad in it!

My Daily Bread

Date:_____

Everything He gives me to do..............He's already provided a way to be done!

Opportunity Given	Provision Provided
_____	_____
_____	_____
_____	_____
_____	_____

Your will be done. Praises & Prayers

Answered

_____ _____
_____ _____
_____ _____
_____ _____

Forgive me as I forgive others.

_____
_____
_____
_____

Character building moments in my refining process.

_____
_____
_____

Filter my feelings through the truth of Your Word.

_____
_____

This is the day that the Lord has made......I will rejoice and be glad in it!

My Daily Bread

Date:_____

Everything He gives me to do..............He's already provided a way to be done!

Opportunity Given	Provision Provided
_____	_____
_____	_____
_____	_____
_____	_____

Your will be done. Praises & Prayers

Answered

Forgive me as I forgive others.

Character building moments in my refining process.

Filter my feelings through the truth of Your Word.

This is the day that the Lord has made......I will rejoice and be glad in it!

My Daily Bread

Date:_____

Everything He gives me to do..............He's already provided a way to be done!

Opportunity Given   Provision Provided

Your will be done. Praises & Prayers

Answered

Forgive me as I forgive others.

Character building moments in my refining process.

Filter my feelings through the truth of Your Word.

This is the day that the Lord has made......I will rejoice and be glad in it!

My Daily Bread

Date:_____

Everything He gives me to do..............He's already provided a way to be done!

Opportunity Given	Provision Provided
_____	_____
_____	_____
_____	_____
_____	_____

Your will be done. Praises & Prayers

Answered

_____ _____

_____ _____

_____ _____

_____ _____

Forgive me as I forgive others.

_____

_____

_____

Character building moments in my refining process.

_____

_____

_____

Filter my feelings through the truth of Your Word.

_____

_____

This is the day that the Lord has made......I will rejoice and be glad in it!

My Daily Bread

Date:_____

Everything He gives me to do..............He's already provided a way to be done!

Opportunity Given	Provision Provided
_____	_____
_____	_____
_____	_____
_____	_____

Your will be done. Praises & Prayers

Answered

____ _____

____ _____

____ _____

____ _____

Forgive me as I forgive others.

_____

_____

_____

Character building moments in my refining process.

_____

_____

_____

Filter my feelings through the truth of Your Word.

_____

_____

This is the day that the Lord has made......I will rejoice and be glad in it!

My Daily Bread

Date:_____

Everything He gives me to do..............He's already provided a way to be done!

Opportunity Given	Provision Provided
_____	_____
_____	_____
_____	_____
_____	_____

Your will be done. Praises & Prayers

Answered

_____   _____

_____   _____

_____   _____

_____   _____

Forgive me as I forgive others.

Character building moments in my refining process.

Filter my feelings through the truth of Your Word.

This is the day that the Lord has made......I will rejoice and be glad in it!

My Daily Bread

Date:_____

Everything He gives me to do..............He's already provided a way to be done!

Opportunity Given	Provision Provided
_____	_____
_____	_____
_____	_____
_____	_____

Your will be done. Praises & Prayers

Answered

Forgive me as I forgive others.

Character building moments in my refining process.

Filter my feelings through the truth of Your Word.

This is the day that the Lord has made......I will rejoice and be glad in it!

My Daily Bread

Date:_____

Everything He gives me to do...............He's already provided a way to be done!

Opportunity Given	Provision Provided
_____	_____
_____	_____
_____	_____
_____	_____

Your will be done. Praises & Prayers

Answered

_____	_____
_____	_____
_____	_____
_____	_____

Forgive me as I forgive others.

_____

_____

_____

Character building moments in my refining process.

_____

_____

_____

Filter my feelings through the truth of Your Word.

_____

_____

This is the day that the Lord has made......I will rejoice and be glad in it!

My Daily Bread

Date:_____

Everything He gives me to do..............He's already provided a way to be done!

Opportunity Given	Provision Provided
_____	_____
_____	_____
_____	_____
_____	_____

Your will be done. Praises & Prayers

Answered

_____ _____
_____ _____
_____ _____
_____ _____

Forgive me as I forgive others.

_____
_____
_____

Character building moments in my refining process.

_____
_____
_____

Filter my feelings through the truth of Your Word.

_____
_____

This is the day that the Lord has made......I will rejoice and be glad in it!

My Daily Bread

Date:_____

Everything He gives me to do..............He's already provided a way to be done!

Opportunity Given	Provision Provided
_____	_____
_____	_____
_____	_____
_____	_____

Your will be done. Praises & Prayers

Answered

_____	_____
_____	_____
_____	_____
_____	_____

Forgive me as I forgive others.

_____
_____
_____

Character building moments in my refining process.

_____
_____
_____

Filter my feelings through the truth of Your Word.

_____
_____

This is the day that the Lord has made......I will rejoice and be glad in it!

My Daily Bread

Date:_____

Everything He gives me to do..............He's already provided a way to be done!

Opportunity Given	Provision Provided

Your will be done. Praises & Prayers

Answered

Forgive me as I forgive others.

Character building moments in my refining process.

Filter my feelings through the truth of Your Word.

This is the day that the Lord has made......I will rejoice and be glad in it!

My Daily Bread

Date:_____

Everything He gives me to do..............He's already provided a way to be done!

Opportunity Given	Provision Provided
_____	_____
_____	_____
_____	_____
_____	_____

Your will be done. Praises & Prayers

Answered

_____ _____
_____ _____
_____ _____
_____ _____

Forgive me as I forgive others.

_____
_____
_____
_____

Character building moments in my refining process.

_____
_____
_____

Filter my feelings through the truth of Your Word.

_____
_____

This is the day that the Lord has made......I will rejoice and be glad in it!

My Daily Bread

Date:_____

Everything He gives me to do..............He's already provided a way to be done!

Opportunity Given	Provision Provided
_____	_____
_____	_____
_____	_____
_____	_____

Your will be done. Praises & Prayers

Answered

_____ _____
_____ _____
_____ _____
_____ _____

Forgive me as I forgive others.

_____
_____
_____

Character building moments in my refining process.

_____
_____
_____

Filter my feelings through the truth of Your Word.

_____
_____

This is the day that the Lord has made......I will rejoice and be glad in it!

My Daily Bread

Everything He gives me to do..............He's already provided a way to be done!

Opportunity Given	Provision Provided
_____	_____
_____	_____
_____	_____
_____	_____

Your will be done. Praises & Prayers

Answered

_____ _____
_____ _____
_____ _____
_____ _____

Forgive me as I forgive others.

_____
_____
_____

Character building moments in my refining process.

_____
_____
_____

Filter my feelings through the truth of Your Word.

_____
_____

This is the day that the Lord has made......I will rejoice and be glad in it!

My Daily Bread

Date:_____

Everything He gives me to do...............He's already provided a way to be done!

Opportunity Given	Provision Provided
_____	_____
_____	_____
_____	_____
_____	_____

Your will be done. Praises & Prayers

Answered

_____ _____

_____ _____

_____ _____

_____ _____

Forgive me as I forgive others.

_____

_____

_____

_____

Character building moments in my refining process.

_____

_____

_____

Filter my feelings through the truth of Your Word.

_____

_____

This is the day that the Lord has made......I will rejoice and be glad in it!

My Daily Bread

Date:_____

Everything He gives me to do...............He's already provided a way to be done!

Opportunity Given	Provision Provided
_____	_____
_____	_____
_____	_____
_____	_____

Your will be done. Praises & Prayers

Answered

_____ _____

_____ _____

_____ _____

_____ _____

Forgive me as I forgive others.

_____

_____

_____

Character building moments in my refining process.

_____

_____

_____

Filter my feelings through the truth of Your Word.

_____

_____

This is the day that the Lord has made......I will rejoice and be glad in it!

My Daily Bread

Date:_____

Everything He gives me to do..............He's already provided a way to be done!

Opportunity Given	Provision Provided

Your will be done. Praises & Prayers

Answered

Forgive me as I forgive others.

Character building moments in my refining process.

Filter my feelings through the truth of Your Word.

This is the day that the Lord has made......I will rejoice and be glad in it!

My Daily Bread

Everything He gives me to do..............He's already provided a way to be done!

Opportunity Given	Provision Provided
_____	_____
_____	_____
_____	_____
_____	

Your will be done. Praises & Prayers

Answered

_____ _____

_____ _____

_____ _____

_____ _____

Forgive me as I forgive others.

Character building moments in my refining process.

Filter my feelings through the truth of Your Word.

This is the day that the Lord has made......I will rejoice and be glad in it!

Notes

KINDNESS

THE GODLY CHARACTER OF KINDNESS

For this very reason, make every effort to add to your faith goodness; and to goodness, knowledge; and to knowledge, self-control; and to self-control, perseverance; and to perseverance, godliness; and to godliness, brotherly kindness; and to brotherly kindness, love. For if you possess these qualities in increasing measure, they will keep you from being ineffective and unproductive in your knowledge of our Lord Jesus Christ.

2 Peter 1: 5-8

What does biblical kindness look like? The simple answer is Jesus. Kindness is selfless, compassionate, and merciful which perfectly describe the heart and actions of our Savior. He made time to meet those in need and even went out of His way to make sure their paths crossed. No one was too far gone to receive the kindness and grace that He offered.

Godly kindness requires us to intentionally seek out ways to make a difference in the lives of others; especially those we may feel don't deserve it. It's in those moments that we need to ask ourselves, "What would Jesus do?" Our honest responses to that question will bring us to a selfless, loving and gracious answer.

Kindness, if practiced daily, will eventually become a habit and a lifestyle. We will begin to look for opportunities to walk alongside Jesus, being His hands and feet, to reach a world in need one person at a time, right where they are.

Because of the kindness of Jesus, the woman at the well came to know Him as her Lord and Savior. She then told her entire village about Him, inviting them to come and meet the One who changed her life. Within a few days many other lives were changed for eternity as they too were saved. One act of kindness leads to another and then another. The possibilities are endless for what God can and will do when you choose to be kind.

BREAD FOR YOUR JOURNEY
GOD'S WORD CONCERNING KINDNESS

Be kind and compassionate to one another, forgiving each other, just as in Christ God forgave you.

Ephesians 4:32

Do to others as you would have them do to you.

Luke 6:31

Therefore, as God's chosen people, holy and dearly loved, clothe yourselves with compassion, kindness, humility, gentleness and patience.

Colossians 3:12

From a wise mind comes wise speech; the words of the wise are persuasive. Kind words are like honey - sweet to the soul and healthy for the body.

Proverbs 16:23-24

Those who pursue righteousness and kindness will find life, righteousness, and honor.

Proverbs 21:21

Blessed are the merciful for they shall obtain mercy.

Matthew 5:7

He who despises his neighbor sins, but blessed is he who is kind to the needy.

Proverbs 14:21

But when the kindness and love of God our Savior appeared, he saved us, not because of righteous things we had done, but because of his mercy. He saved us through the washing of rebirth and renewal by the Holy Spirit.

Titus 3:4-5

Checkpoints Along The Way

Expectations: What would change in my life if I had more Kindness?

_____

_____

_____

_____

_____

Memorable Moments: What happened when I put Kindness into practice?

_____

_____

_____

_____

_____

Reaping A Harvest: How has my life improved because of Kindness?

_____

_____

_____

_____

_____

My Daily Bread   Date:_____

Everything He gives me to do..............He's already provided a way to be done!

Opportunity Given	Provision Provided
_____	_____
_____	_____
_____	_____
_____	_____

Your will be done. Praises & Prayers

Answered

_____ _____
_____ _____
_____ _____
_____ _____

Forgive me as I forgive others.

_____
_____
_____

Character building moments in my refining process.

_____
_____
_____

Filter my feelings through the truth of Your Word.

_____
_____

This is the day that the Lord has made......I will rejoice and be glad in it!

My Daily Bread

Date:_____

Everything He gives me to do..............He's already provided a way to be done!

Opportunity Given	Provision Provided
_____	_____
_____	_____
_____	_____
_____	_____

Your will be done. Praises & Prayers

Answered

_____ _____

_____ _____

_____ _____

_____ _____

Forgive me as I forgive others.

_____

_____

_____

Character building moments in my refining process.

_____

_____

_____

Filter my feelings through the truth of Your Word.

_____

_____

This is the day that the Lord has made......I will rejoice and be glad in it!

My Daily Bread

Date:_____

Everything He gives me to do..............He's already provided a way to be done!

Opportunity Given	Provision Provided
_____	_____
_____	_____
_____	_____
_____	_____

Your will be done. Praises & Prayers

Answered

_____ _____

_____ _____

_____ _____

_____ _____

Forgive me as I forgive others.

Character building moments in my refining process.

Filter my feelings through the truth of Your Word.

This is the day that the Lord has made......I will rejoice and be glad in it!

My Daily Bread

Date:_____

Everything He gives me to do..............He's already provided a way to be done!

Opportunity Given	Provision Provided

Your will be done. Praises & Prayers

Answered

Forgive me as I forgive others.

Character building moments in my refining process.

Filter my feelings through the truth of Your Word.

This is the day that the Lord has made......I will rejoice and be glad in it!

My Daily Bread

Date:_____

Everything He gives me to do..............He's already provided a way to be done!

Opportunity Given	Provision Provided
_____	_____
_____	_____
_____	_____
_____	_____

Your will be done. Praises & Prayers

Answered

_____	_____
_____	_____
_____	_____
_____	_____

Forgive me as I forgive others.

_____
_____
_____

Character building moments in my refining process.

_____
_____
_____

Filter my feelings through the truth of Your Word.

_____
_____

This is the day that the Lord has made......I will rejoice and be glad in it!

My Daily Bread

Date:_____

Everything He gives me to do..............He's already provided a way to be done!

Opportunity Given	Provision Provided
_____	_____
_____	_____
_____	_____
_____	_____

Your will be done. Praises & Prayers

Answered

_____ _____

_____ _____

_____ _____

_____ _____

Forgive me as I forgive others.

_____

_____

_____

Character building moments in my refining process.

_____

_____

_____

Filter my feelings through the truth of Your Word.

_____

_____

This is the day that the Lord has made......I will rejoice and be glad in it!

My Daily Bread

Date:_____

Everything He gives me to do..............He's already provided a way to be done!

Opportunity Given	Provision Provided
_____	_____
_____	_____
_____	_____
_____	_____

Your will be done. Praises & Prayers

Answered

_____	_____
_____	_____
_____	_____
_____	_____

Forgive me as I forgive others.

_____
_____
_____
_____

Character building moments in my refining process.

_____
_____
_____

Filter my feelings through the truth of Your Word.

_____
_____

This is the day that the Lord has made......I will rejoice and be glad in it!

My Daily Bread

Date:_____

Everything He gives me to do..............He's already provided a way to be done!

Opportunity Given	Provision Provided
_____	_____
_____	_____
_____	_____
_____	_____

Your will be done. Praises & Prayers

Answered

_____ _____

_____ _____

_____ _____

_____ _____

Forgive me as I forgive others.

_____
_____
_____

Character building moments in my refining process.

_____
_____
_____

Filter my feelings through the truth of Your Word.

_____
_____

This is the day that the Lord has made......I will rejoice and be glad in it!

My Daily Bread

Date:_____

Everything He gives me to do..............He's already provided a way to be done!

Opportunity Given	Provision Provided
_____	_____
_____	_____
_____	_____
_____	_____

Your will be done. Praises & Prayers

Answered

_____ _____
_____ _____
_____ _____
_____ _____

Forgive me as I forgive others.

_____
_____
_____
_____

Character building moments in my refining process.

_____
_____
_____

Filter my feelings through the truth of Your Word.

_____
_____

This is the day that the Lord has made......I will rejoice and be glad in it!

My Daily Bread

Date:_____

Everything He gives me to do..............He's already provided a way to be done!

Opportunity Given	Provision Provided
_____	_____
_____	_____
_____	_____
_____	_____

Your will be done. Praises & Prayers

Answered

_____

_____

_____

_____

Forgive me as I forgive others.

Character building moments in my refining process.

Filter my feelings through the truth of Your Word.

This is the day that the Lord has made......I will rejoice and be glad in it!

My Daily Bread

Date:_____

Everything He gives me to do..............He's already provided a way to be done!

Opportunity Given	Provision Provided
_____	_____
_____	_____
_____	_____
_____	_____

Your will be done. Praises & Prayers

Answered

_____ _____
_____ _____
_____ _____
_____ _____

Forgive me as I forgive others.

_____
_____
_____

Character building moments in my refining process.

_____
_____
_____

Filter my feelings through the truth of Your Word.

_____
_____

This is the day that the Lord has made......I will rejoice and be glad in it!

My Daily Bread

Date:_____

Everything He gives me to do..............He's already provided a way to be done!

Opportunity Given   Provision Provided

_____   _____

_____   _____

_____   _____

_____   _____

Your will be done. Praises & Prayers

Answered

_____   _____

_____   _____

_____   _____

_____   _____

Forgive me as I forgive others.

_____

_____

_____

Character building moments in my refining process.

_____

_____

_____

Filter my feelings through the truth of Your Word.

_____

_____

This is the day that the Lord has made......I will rejoice and be glad in it!

My Daily Bread

Date:_____

Everything He gives me to do..............He's already provided a way to be done!

Opportunity Given	Provision Provided
_____	_____
_____	_____
_____	_____
_____	_____

Your will be done. Praises & Prayers

Answered

Forgive me as I forgive others.

Character building moments in my refining process.

Filter my feelings through the truth of Your Word.

This is the day that the Lord has made......I will rejoice and be glad in it!

My Daily Bread

Date:_____

Everything He gives me to do..............He's already provided a way to be done!

Opportunity Given	Provision Provided
_____	_____
_____	_____
_____	_____
_____	_____

Your will be done. Praises & Prayers

Answered

_____ _____

_____ _____

_____ _____

_____ _____

Forgive me as I forgive others.

_____

_____

_____

Character building moments in my refining process.

_____

_____

_____

Filter my feelings through the truth of Your Word.

_____

_____

This is the day that the Lord has made......I will rejoice and be glad in it!

My Daily Bread

Date:_____

Everything He gives me to do...............He's already provided a way to be done!

Opportunity Given	Provision Provided
_____	_____
_____	_____
_____	_____
_____	_____

Your will be done. Praises & Prayers

Answered

_____ _____
_____ _____
_____ _____
_____ _____

Forgive me as I forgive others.

_____
_____
_____

Character building moments in my refining process.

_____
_____
_____

Filter my feelings through the truth of Your Word.

_____
_____

This is the day that the Lord has made......I will rejoice and be glad in it!

My Daily Bread

Date:_____

Everything He gives me to do...............He's already provided a way to be done!

Opportunity Given	Provision Provided
_____	_____
_____	_____
_____	_____
_____	_____

Your will be done. Praises & Prayers

Answered

_____ _____
_____ _____
_____ _____
_____ _____

Forgive me as I forgive others.

_____
_____
_____
_____

Character building moments in my refining process.

_____
_____
_____

Filter my feelings through the truth of Your Word.

_____
_____

This is the day that the Lord has made......I will rejoice and be glad in it!

My Daily Bread   Date:_____

Everything He gives me to do..............He's already provided a way to be done!

Opportunity Given	Provision Provided
_____	_____
_____	_____
_____	_____
_____	_____

Your will be done. Praises & Prayers

Answered

_____   _____

_____   _____

_____   _____

_____   _____

Forgive me as I forgive others.

_____
_____
_____
_____

Character building moments in my refining process.

_____
_____
_____

Filter my feelings through the truth of Your Word.

_____
_____

This is the day that the Lord has made......I will rejoice and be glad in it!

My Daily Bread

Date:_____

Everything He gives me to do..............He's already provided a way to be done!

Opportunity Given	Provision Provided

Your will be done. Praises & Prayers

Answered

Forgive me as I forgive others.

Character building moments in my refining process.

Filter my feelings through the truth of Your Word.

This is the day that the Lord has made......I will rejoice and be glad in it!

My Daily Bread

Date:_____

Everything He gives me to do..............He's already provided a way to be done!

Opportunity Given	Provision Provided
_____	_____
_____	_____
_____	_____
_____	_____

Your will be done. Praises & Prayers

Answered

_____   _____

_____   _____

_____   _____

_____   _____

Forgive me as I forgive others.

_____

_____

_____

Character building moments in my refining process.

_____

_____

_____

Filter my feelings through the truth of Your Word.

_____

_____

This is the day that the Lord has made......I will rejoice and be glad in it!

My Daily Bread

Date:_____

Everything He gives me to do..............He's already provided a way to be done!

Opportunity Given   Provision Provided

_____   _____

_____   _____

_____   _____

_____   _____

Your will be done. Praises & Prayers

Answered

_____   _____

_____   _____

_____   _____

_____   _____

Forgive me as I forgive others.

_____

_____

_____

Character building moments in my refining process.

_____

_____

_____

Filter my feelings through the truth of Your Word.

_____

_____

This is the day that the Lord has made......I will rejoice and be glad in it!

My Daily Bread

Date:_____

Everything He gives me to do..............He's already provided a way to be done!

Opportunity Given	Provision Provided
_____	_____
_____	_____
_____	_____
_____	_____

Your will be done. Praises & Prayers

Answered

_____
_____
_____
_____

Forgive me as I forgive others.

Character building moments in my refining process.

Filter my feelings through the truth of Your Word.

This is the day that the Lord has made......I will rejoice and be glad in it!

My Daily Bread

Date:_____

Everything He gives me to do..............He's already provided a way to be done!

Opportunity Given	Provision Provided
_____	_____
_____	_____
_____	_____
_____	_____

Your will be done. Praises & Prayers

Answered

_____ _____

_____ _____

_____ _____

_____ _____

Forgive me as I forgive others.

_____

_____

_____

Character building moments in my refining process.

_____

_____

_____

Filter my feelings through the truth of Your Word.

_____

_____

This is the day that the Lord has made......I will rejoice and be glad in it!

My Daily Bread

Date:_____

Everything He gives me to do..............He's already provided a way to be done!

Opportunity Given	Provision Provided
_____	_____
_____	_____
_____	_____
_____	_____

Your will be done. Praises & Prayers

Answered

____ _____

____ _____

____ _____

____ _____

Forgive me as I forgive others.

_____

_____

_____

_____

Character building moments in my refining process.

_____

_____

_____

Filter my feelings through the truth of Your Word.

_____

_____

This is the day that the Lord has made......I will rejoice and be glad in it!

My Daily Bread

Date:_____

Everything He gives me to do..............He's already provided a way to be done!

Opportunity Given   Provision Provided

_____   _____

_____   _____

_____   _____

_____   _____

Your will be done. Praises & Prayers

Answered

_____   _____

_____   _____

_____   _____

_____   _____

Forgive me as I forgive others.

_____

_____

_____

Character building moments in my refining process.

_____

_____

Filter my feelings through the truth of Your Word.

_____

_____

This is the day that the Lord has made......I will rejoice and be glad in it!

My Daily Bread

Date:_____

Everything He gives me to do...............He's already provided a way to be done!

Opportunity Given	Provision Provided
_____	_____
_____	_____
_____	_____
_____	_____

Your will be done. Praises & Prayers

Answered

_____	_____
_____	_____
_____	_____
_____	_____

Forgive me as I forgive others.

_____
_____
_____
_____

Character building moments in my refining process.

_____
_____
_____

Filter my feelings through the truth of Your Word.

_____
_____

This is the day that the Lord has made......I will rejoice and be glad in it!

My Daily Bread

Date:_____

Everything He gives me to do..............He's already provided a way to be done!

Opportunity Given   Provision Provided

_____   _____

_____   _____

_____   _____

_____   _____

Your will be done. Praises & Prayers

Answered

_____   _____

_____   _____

_____   _____

_____   _____

Forgive me as I forgive others.

_____

_____

_____

Character building moments in my refining process.

_____

_____

_____

Filter my feelings through the truth of Your Word.

_____

_____

This is the day that the Lord has made......I will rejoice and be glad in it!

My Daily Bread

Date:_____

Everything He gives me to do..............He's already provided a way to be done!

Opportunity Given	Provision Provided
_____	_____
_____	_____
_____	_____
_____	_____

Your will be done. Praises & Prayers

Answered

___ _____
___ _____
___ _____
___ _____

Forgive me as I forgive others.

_____
_____
_____

Character building moments in my refining process.

_____
_____
_____

Filter my feelings through the truth of Your Word.

_____
_____

This is the day that the Lord has made......I will rejoice and be glad in it!

My Daily Bread

Date:_____

Everything He gives me to do..............He's already provided a way to be done!

Opportunity Given	Provision Provided
_____	_____
_____	_____
_____	_____
_____	_____

Your will be done. Praises & Prayers

Answered

_____ _____

_____ _____

_____ _____

_____ _____

Forgive me as I forgive others.

_____

_____

_____

Character building moments in my refining process.

_____

_____

_____

Filter my feelings through the truth of Your Word.

_____

_____

This is the day that the Lord has made......I will rejoice and be glad in it!

My Daily Bread

Date:_____

Everything He gives me to do..............He's already provided a way to be done!

Opportunity Given	Provision Provided
_____	_____
_____	_____
_____	_____

Your will be done. Praises & Prayers

Answered

_____   _____
_____   _____
_____   _____
_____   _____

Forgive me as I forgive others.

_____
_____
_____

Character building moments in my refining process.

_____
_____
_____

Filter my feelings through the truth of Your Word.

_____
_____

This is the day that the Lord has made......I will rejoice and be glad in it!

My Daily Bread

Date:_____

Everything He gives me to do..............He's already provided a way to be done!

Opportunity Given	Provision Provided

Your will be done. Praises & Prayers

Answered

Forgive me as I forgive others.

Character building moments in my refining process.

Filter my feelings through the truth of Your Word.

This is the day that the Lord has made.......I will rejoice and be glad in it!

My Daily Bread

Date:_____

Everything He gives me to do..............He's already provided a way to be done!

Opportunity Given	Provision Provided
_____	_____
_____	_____
_____	_____
_____	_____

Your will be done. Praises & Prayers

Answered

_____ _____

_____ _____

_____ _____

_____ _____

Forgive me as I forgive others.

_____
_____
_____
_____

Character building moments in my refining process.

_____
_____
_____

Filter my feelings through the truth of Your Word.

_____
_____

This is the day that the Lord has made......I will rejoice and be glad in it!

Notes

GOODNESS

THE GODLY CHARACTER OF GOODNESS

Our purpose is to do what is right, not only in the sight
of the Lord, but also in the sight of others.

2 Corinthians 8:21

Goodness is the quality of being virtuous or morally good. It's associated with integrity and honesty as we do what is right, regardless of who's watching and encouraging others to do the same.

When Potiphar's wife tried to seduce Joseph, his response demonstrated his desire to live a virtuous and morally good life. He acknowledged that this sin would be both wicked and directly against God. His integrity gave him the courage to verbally refuse and to physically run from the temptation. It was Joseph's heart to honor God that kept him pure.

As believers in Christ, our past sins have been wiped away by the precious blood of Jesus and we've been given a new life in Him as new creations. This new life provides the opportunity to live a life that honors God by living with integrity, honesty and purity.

When we make the decision ahead of time to live a life of goodness, we are better able to handle situations that will arise and test our integrity. Our commitment to God to live a life that honors Him will give us the wisdom and courage to stand when temptations come.

When the Godly fruit of Goodness is displayed in our lives, we refuse to spread gossip, watch distasteful movies and TV shows or participate in inappropriate relationships. Our desire is to flee from the things that will hinder our relationship with God and tempt us to sin. This desire comes from a grateful heart that has experienced the goodness, mercy and grace of our loving Savior.

BREAD FOR YOUR JOURNEY
GOD'S WORD CONCERNING GOODNESS

Therefore, as we have opportunity, let us do good to all people, especially to those who belong to the family of believers.

Galatians 6:10

Love must be sincere. Hate what is evil; cling to what is good.

Romans 12:9

Do not be overcome by evil, but overcome evil with good.

Romans 12:21

Neither do you light a lamp, and put it under a measuring basket, but on a stand; and it shines to all who are in the house. Even so, let your light shine before men; that they may see your good works, and glorify your Father who is in heaven.

Matthew 5:15-16

Do not let any unwholesome talk come out of your mouths, but only what is helpful for building others up according to their needs, that it may benefit those who listen.

Ephesians 4:29

Don't be conformed to this world, but be transformed by the renewing of your mind, so that you may prove what is the good, well-pleasing, and perfect will of God.

Romans 12:2

Give thanks to the Lord, for he is good; His love endures forever.

1 Chronicles 16:34

Checkpoints Along The Way

Expectations: What would change in my life if I had more Goodness?

_____

_____

_____

_____

_____

Memorable Moments: What happened when I put Goodness into practice?

_____

_____

_____

_____

_____

Reaping A Harvest: How has my life improved because of Goodness?

_____

_____

_____

_____

_____

My Daily Bread

Date:_____

Everything He gives me to do..............He's already provided a way to be done!

Opportunity Given	Provision Provided
_____	_____
_____	_____
_____	_____
_____	_____

Your will be done. Praises & Prayers

Answered

_____ _____

_____ _____

_____ _____

_____ _____

Forgive me as I forgive others.

Character building moments in my refining process.

Filter my feelings through the truth of Your Word.

This is the day that the Lord has made......I will rejoice and be glad in it!

My Daily Bread

Date:_____

Everything He gives me to do..............He's already provided a way to be done!

Opportunity Given   Provision Provided

_____   _____

_____   _____

_____   _____

_____   _____

Your will be done. Praises & Prayers

Answered

_____   _____

_____   _____

_____   _____

_____   _____

Forgive me as I forgive others.

_____

_____

_____

Character building moments in my refining process.

_____

_____

_____

Filter my feelings through the truth of Your Word.

_____

_____

This is the day that the Lord has made......I will rejoice and be glad in it!

My Daily Bread

Date:_____

Everything He gives me to do..............He's already provided a way to be done!

Opportunity Given	Provision Provided
_____	_____
_____	_____
_____	_____
_____	_____

Your will be done. Praises & Prayers

Answered

_____	_____
_____	_____
_____	_____
_____	_____

Forgive me as I forgive others.

_____

_____

_____

Character building moments in my refining process.

_____

_____

_____

Filter my feelings through the truth of Your Word.

_____

_____

This is the day that the Lord has made......I will rejoice and be glad in it!

My Daily Bread

Everything He gives me to do..............He's already provided a way to be done!

Opportunity Given	Provision Provided
_____	_____
_____	_____
_____	_____
_____	_____

Your will be done. Praises & Prayers

Answered

_____ _____
_____ _____
_____ _____
_____ _____

Forgive me as I forgive others.

_____
_____
_____

Character building moments in my refining process.

_____
_____
_____

Filter my feelings through the truth of Your Word.

_____
_____

This is the day that the Lord has made......I will rejoice and be glad in it!

My Daily Bread

Date:_____

Everything He gives me to do..............He's already provided a way to be done!

Opportunity Given	Provision Provided
_____	_____
_____	_____
_____	_____
_____	_____

Your will be done. Praises & Prayers

Answered

_____ _____

_____ _____

_____ _____

_____ _____

Forgive me as I forgive others.

Character building moments in my refining process.

Filter my feelings through the truth of Your Word.

This is the day that the Lord has made......I will rejoice and be glad in it!

My Daily Bread

Date:_____

Everything He gives me to do..............He's already provided a way to be done!

Opportunity Given   Provision Provided

Your will be done. Praises & Prayers

Answered

Forgive me as I forgive others.

Character building moments in my refining process.

Filter my feelings through the truth of Your Word.

This is the day that the Lord has made......I will rejoice and be glad in it!

My Daily Bread

Date:_____

Everything He gives me to do..............He's already provided a way to be done!

Opportunity Given	Provision Provided
_____	_____
_____	_____
_____	_____
_____	_____

Your will be done. Praises & Prayers

Answered

_____	_____
_____	_____
_____	_____
_____	_____

Forgive me as I forgive others.

_____
_____
_____

Character building moments in my refining process.

_____
_____
_____

Filter my feelings through the truth of Your Word.

_____
_____

This is the day that the Lord has made......I will rejoice and be glad in it!

My Daily Bread

Date:_____

Everything He gives me to do..............He's already provided a way to be done!

Opportunity Given	Provision Provided
_____	_____
_____	_____
_____	_____
_____	_____

Your will be done. Praises & Prayers

Answered

_____ _____

_____ _____

_____ _____

_____ _____

Forgive me as I forgive others.

_____

_____

_____

Character building moments in my refining process.

_____

_____

_____

Filter my feelings through the truth of Your Word.

_____

_____

This is the day that the Lord has made......I will rejoice and be glad in it!

My Daily Bread

Date:_____

Everything He gives me to do..............He's already provided a way to be done!

Opportunity Given	Provision Provided
_____	_____
_____	_____
_____	_____
_____	_____

Your will be done. Praises & Prayers

Answered

_____	_____
_____	_____
_____	_____
_____	_____

Forgive me as I forgive others.

Character building moments in my refining process.

Filter my feelings through the truth of Your Word.

This is the day that the Lord has made......I will rejoice and be glad in it!

My Daily Bread

Date:_____

Everything He gives me to do..............He's already provided a way to be done!

Opportunity Given	Provision Provided
_____	_____
_____	_____
_____	_____
_____	_____

Your will be done. Praises & Prayers

Answered

Forgive me as I forgive others.

Character building moments in my refining process.

Filter my feelings through the truth of Your Word.

This is the day that the Lord has made......I will rejoice and be glad in it!

My Daily Bread

Date:_____

Everything He gives me to do..............He's already provided a way to be done!

Opportunity Given	Provision Provided
_____	_____
_____	_____
_____	_____
_____	_____

Your will be done. Praises & Prayers

Answered

_____ _____
_____ _____
_____ _____
_____ _____

Forgive me as I forgive others.

_____
_____
_____

Character building moments in my refining process.

_____
_____
_____

Filter my feelings through the truth of Your Word.

_____
_____

This is the day that the Lord has made......I will rejoice and be glad in it!

My Daily Bread

Date:_____

Everything He gives me to do..............He's already provided a way to be done!

Opportunity Given   Provision Provided

_____   _____

_____   _____

_____   _____

_____   _____

Your will be done. Praises & Prayers

Answered

_____   _____

_____   _____

_____   _____

_____   _____

Forgive me as I forgive others.

_____

_____

_____

Character building moments in my refining process.

_____

_____

Filter my feelings through the truth of Your Word.

_____

_____

This is the day that the Lord has made......I will rejoice and be glad in it!

My Daily Bread

Date:_____

Everything He gives me to do..............He's already provided a way to be done!

Opportunity Given	Provision Provided
_____	_____
_____	_____
_____	_____
_____	_____

Your will be done. Praises & Prayers

Answered

_____ _____

_____ _____

_____ _____

_____ _____

Forgive me as I forgive others.

_____
_____
_____

Character building moments in my refining process.

_____
_____
_____

Filter my feelings through the truth of Your Word.

_____
_____

This is the day that the Lord has made......I will rejoice and be glad in it!

My Daily Bread

Date:_____

Everything He gives me to do...............He's already provided a way to be done!

Opportunity Given	Provision Provided
_____	_____
_____	_____
_____	_____
_____	_____

Your will be done. Praises & Prayers

Answered

_____ _____

_____ _____

_____ _____

_____ _____

Forgive me as I forgive others.

_____

_____

_____

Character building moments in my refining process.

_____

_____

_____

Filter my feelings through the truth of Your Word.

_____

_____

This is the day that the Lord has made......I will rejoice and be glad in it!

My Daily Bread

Date:_____

Everything He gives me to do..............He's already provided a way to be done!

Opportunity Given	Provision Provided
_____	_____
_____	_____
_____	_____
_____	_____

Your will be done. Praises & Prayers

Answered

_____	_____
_____	_____
_____	_____
_____	_____

Forgive me as I forgive others.

_____
_____
_____

Character building moments in my refining process.

_____
_____
_____

Filter my feelings through the truth of Your Word.

_____
_____

This is the day that the Lord has made......I will rejoice and be glad in it!

My Daily Bread

Date:_____

Everything He gives me to do...............He's already provided a way to be done!

Opportunity Given	Provision Provided
_____	_____
_____	_____
_____	_____
_____	_____

Your will be done. Praises & Prayers

Answered

_____ _____

_____ _____

_____ _____

_____ _____

Forgive me as I forgive others.

_____
_____
_____

Character building moments in my refining process.

_____
_____
_____

Filter my feelings through the truth of Your Word.

_____
_____

This is the day that the Lord has made......I will rejoice and be glad in it!

My Daily Bread

Date:_____

Everything He gives me to do..............He's already provided a way to be done!

Opportunity Given	Provision Provided

Your will be done. Praises & Prayers

Answered

Forgive me as I forgive others.

Character building moments in my refining process.

Filter my feelings through the truth of Your Word.

This is the day that the Lord has made......I will rejoice and be glad in it!

My Daily Bread

Date:_____

Everything He gives me to do..............He's already provided a way to be done!

Opportunity Given	Provision Provided
_____	_____
_____	_____
_____	_____
_____	_____

Your will be done. Praises & Prayers

Answered

_____ _____
_____ _____
_____ _____
_____ _____

Forgive me as I forgive others.

_____
_____
_____

Character building moments in my refining process.

_____
_____
_____

Filter my feelings through the truth of Your Word.

_____
_____

This is the day that the Lord has made......I will rejoice and be glad in it!

My Daily Bread

Date:_____

Everything He gives me to do..............He's already provided a way to be done!

Opportunity Given	Provision Provided
_____	_____
_____	_____
_____	_____
_____	_____

Your will be done. Praises & Prayers

Answered

_____ _____

_____ _____

_____ _____

_____ _____

Forgive me as I forgive others.

Character building moments in my refining process.

Filter my feelings through the truth of Your Word.

This is the day that the Lord has made......I will rejoice and be glad in it!

My Daily Bread

Date:_____

Everything He gives me to do..............He's already provided a way to be done!

Opportunity Given	Provision Provided
_____	_____
_____	_____
_____	_____
_____	_____

Your will be done. Praises & Prayers

Answered

_____ _____

_____ _____

_____ _____

_____ _____

Forgive me as I forgive others.

_____

_____

_____

Character building moments in my refining process.

_____

_____

_____

Filter my feelings through the truth of Your Word.

_____

_____

This is the day that the Lord has made......I will rejoice and be glad in it!

My Daily Bread

Date:_____

Everything He gives me to do...............He's already provided a way to be done!

Opportunity Given	Provision Provided
_____	_____
_____	_____
_____	_____
_____	_____

Your will be done. Praises & Prayers

Answered

_____ _____

_____ _____

_____ _____

_____ _____

Forgive me as I forgive others.

_____

_____

_____

Character building moments in my refining process.

_____

_____

_____

Filter my feelings through the truth of Your Word.

_____

_____

This is the day that the Lord has made......I will rejoice and be glad in it!

My Daily Bread

Date:_____

Everything He gives me to do..............He's already provided a way to be done!

Opportunity Given	Provision Provided
_____	_____
_____	_____
_____	_____
_____	_____

Your will be done. Praises & Prayers

Answered

Forgive me as I forgive others.

Character building moments in my refining process.

Filter my feelings through the truth of Your Word.

This is the day that the Lord has made......I will rejoice and be glad in it!

My Daily Bread

Date:_____

Everything He gives me to do..............He's already provided a way to be done!

Opportunity Given	Provision Provided
_____	_____
_____	_____
_____	_____
_____	_____

Your will be done. Praises & Prayers

Answered

_____ _____
_____ _____
_____ _____
_____ _____

Forgive me as I forgive others.

_____
_____
_____
_____

Character building moments in my refining process.

_____
_____
_____

Filter my feelings through the truth of Your Word.

_____
_____

This is the day that the Lord has made......I will rejoice and be glad in it!

My Daily Bread

Date:_____

Everything He gives me to do...............He's already provided a way to be done!

Opportunity Given | Provision Provided

_____ | _____

_____ | _____

_____ | _____

_____ | _____

Your will be done. Praises & Prayers

Answered

_____ | _____

_____ | _____

_____ | _____

_____ | _____

Forgive me as I forgive others.

_____

_____

_____

Character building moments in my refining process.

_____

_____

_____

Filter my feelings through the truth of Your Word.

_____

_____

This is the day that the Lord has made......I will rejoice and be glad in it!

My Daily Bread

Date:_____

Everything He gives me to do..............He's already provided a way to be done!

Opportunity Given	Provision Provided
_____	_____
_____	_____
_____	_____
_____	_____

Your will be done. Praises & Prayers

Answered

_____ _____

_____ _____

_____ _____

_____ _____

Forgive me as I forgive others.

_____
_____
_____
_____

Character building moments in my refining process.

_____
_____
_____

Filter my feelings through the truth of Your Word.

_____
_____

This is the day that the Lord has made......I will rejoice and be glad in it!

My Daily Bread

Date:_____

Everything He gives me to do..............He's already provided a way to be done!

Opportunity Given	Provision Provided
_____	_____
_____	_____
_____	_____
_____	_____

Your will be done. Praises & Prayers

Answered

___ _____
___ _____
___ _____
___ _____

Forgive me as I forgive others.

_____
_____
_____

Character building moments in my refining process.

_____
_____
_____

Filter my feelings through the truth of Your Word.

_____
_____

This is the day that the Lord has made......I will rejoice and be glad in it!

My Daily Bread   Date:_____

Everything He gives me to do..............He's already provided a way to be done!

Opportunity Given   Provision Provided

_____   _____

_____   _____

_____   _____

_____   _____

Your will be done. Praises & Prayers

Answered

_____   _____

_____   _____

_____   _____

_____   _____

Forgive me as I forgive others.

_____

_____

_____

Character building moments in my refining process.

_____

_____

_____

Filter my feelings through the truth of Your Word.

_____

_____

This is the day that the Lord has made......I will rejoice and be glad in it!

My Daily Bread

Date:_____

Everything He gives me to do..............He's already provided a way to be done!

Opportunity Given	Provision Provided

Your will be done. Praises & Prayers

Answered

Forgive me as I forgive others.

Character building moments in my refining process.

Filter my feelings through the truth of Your Word.

This is the day that the Lord has made......I will rejoice and be glad in it!

My Daily Bread

Date:_____

Everything He gives me to do..............He's already provided a way to be done!

Opportunity Given	Provision Provided
_____	_____
_____	_____
_____	_____
_____	_____

Your will be done. Praises & Prayers

Answered

_____ _____

_____ _____

_____ _____

_____ _____

Forgive me as I forgive others.

_____

_____

_____

Character building moments in my refining process.

_____

_____

_____

Filter my feelings through the truth of Your Word.

_____

_____

This is the day that the Lord has made......I will rejoice and be glad in it!

My Daily Bread

Date:_____

Everything He gives me to do..............He's already provided a way to be done!

Opportunity Given	Provision Provided
_____	_____
_____	_____
_____	_____
_____	_____

Your will be done. Praises & Prayers

Answered

_____	_____
_____	_____
_____	_____
_____	_____

Forgive me as I forgive others.

_____
_____
_____

Character building moments in my refining process.

_____
_____
_____

Filter my feelings through the truth of Your Word.

_____
_____

This is the day that the Lord has made......I will rejoice and be glad in it!

My Daily Bread

Date:_____

Everything He gives me to do..............He's already provided a way to be done!

Opportunity Given	Provision Provided
_____	_____
_____	_____
_____	_____
_____	_____

Your will be done. Praises & Prayers

Answered

_____ _____

_____ _____

_____ _____

_____ _____

Forgive me as I forgive others.

_____

_____

_____

_____

Character building moments in my refining process.

_____

_____

_____

Filter my feelings through the truth of Your Word.

_____

_____

This is the day that the Lord has made......I will rejoice and be glad in it!

Notes

FAITHFULNESS

THE GODLY CHARACTER
OF FAITHFULNESS

His master said to him, 'Well done, good and faithful servant. You have been
faithful over a little; I will set you over much. Enter into the joy of your master.

Matthew 25:21

The things we have in life are blessings from God and He has entrusted us
with them. He hasn't given us all the same things. We each have differences in
financial status, health, intellect, skills and talents, etc. No matter how much
or how little, they are all gifts from God and are exactly what is needed for us
to accomplish all He had prepared in advance for us to do.

What will you do with the blessings you've been given as you await the return
of the Lord? Will you use them to help and serve others? Will you keep them
for yourself or even worse bury them by not using them? God's desire is that
we would learn to be faithful stewards and put them to use for His glory.

To do that, we must keep our eyes on Jesus, who leads us and makes our faith
complete. He endured the shame of being nailed to a cross, because He knew that
later on He would be glad He did. Now He is seated at the right hand of the throne
of God. He never lost sight of where He was headed nor should we. The promise of
eternity with Christ should spur us on to faithfully live for Him now. He is worth it!

When we're faithful to God it means that we trust that He will care for us, we
follow where He leads, and we love Him. Faithfulness does not mean that we
will be perfect. It does not mean that we won't struggle or that we won't make
poor decisions. It does mean that we will continue to trust in God and try to
follow His commandments even when life is difficult.

BREAD FOR YOUR JOURNEY
GOD'S WORD CONCERNING FAITHFULNESS

Let us hold on firmly to the confession of our hope without wavering, since he who promised is faithful.

Hebrews 10:23

Because of the Lord's great love we are not consumed, for his mercies never fail. They are new every morning; great is your faithfulness.

Lamentations 3:22-23

The one who calls you is faithful, and he will do it.

1 Thessalonians 5:24

No temptation has seized you except what is common to man. And God is faithful; he will not let you be tempted beyond what you can bear. But when you are tempted, he will also provide a way out so that you can stand up under it.

1 Corinthians 10:13

If we confess our sins, he is faithful and just and will forgive us our sins and purify us from all unrighteousness.

1 John 1:9

The Lord is righteous in all his ways and faithful in all he does.

Psalm 145:17

Even though I walk through the valley of the shadow of death, I will fear no evil, for you are with me; your rod and your staff, they comfort me.

Psalm 23:4

Therefore, since we are surrounded by such a great cloud of witnesses, let us throw off everything that hinders and the sin that so easily entangles. And let us run with perseverance the race marked out for us, fixing our eyes on Jesus, the author and perfecter of faith. Who for the joy set before him he endured the cross, scorning its shame, and sat down at the right hand of the throne of God.

Hebrews 12: 1-2

Checkpoints Along The Way

Expectations: What would change in my life if I had more Faithfulness?

_____

_____

_____

_____

_____

Memorable Moments: What happened when I put Faithfulness into practice?

_____

_____

_____

_____

_____

Reaping A Harvest: How has my life improved because of Faithfulness?

_____

_____

_____

_____

_____

My Daily Bread

Date:_____

Everything He gives me to do...............He's already provided a way to be done!

Opportunity Given	Provision Provided

Your will be done. Praises & Prayers

Answered

Forgive me as I forgive others.

Character building moments in my refining process.

Filter my feelings through the truth of Your Word.

This is the day that the Lord has made......I will rejoice and be glad in it!

My Daily Bread

Date:_____

Everything He gives me to do..............He's already provided a way to be done!

Opportunity Given	Provision Provided
_____	_____
_____	_____
_____	_____
_____	_____

Your will be done. Praises & Prayers

Answered

Forgive me as I forgive others.

Character building moments in my refining process.

Filter my feelings through the truth of Your Word.

This is the day that the Lord has made......I will rejoice and be glad in it!

My Daily Bread

Date:_____

Everything He gives me to do..............He's already provided a way to be done!

Opportunity Given	Provision Provided
_____	_____
_____	_____
_____	_____
_____	_____

Your will be done. Praises & Prayers

Answered

_____   _____

_____   _____

_____   _____

_____   _____

Forgive me as I forgive others.

_____

_____

_____

Character building moments in my refining process.

_____

_____

_____

Filter my feelings through the truth of Your Word.

_____

_____

This is the day that the Lord has made......I will rejoice and be glad in it!

My Daily Bread

Date:_____

Everything He gives me to do..............He's already provided a way to be done!

Opportunity Given   Provision Provided

_____   _____

_____   _____

_____   _____

_____   _____

Your will be done. Praises & Prayers

Answered

_____ _____

_____ _____

_____ _____

_____ _____

Forgive me as I forgive others.

_____

_____

_____

Character building moments in my refining process.

_____

_____

_____

Filter my feelings through the truth of Your Word.

_____

_____

This is the day that the Lord has made......I will rejoice and be glad in it!

My Daily Bread

Date:_____

Everything He gives me to do..............He's already provided a way to be done!

Opportunity Given	Provision Provided
_____	_____
_____	_____
_____	_____
_____	_____

Your will be done. Praises & Prayers

Answered

Forgive me as I forgive others.

Character building moments in my refining process.

Filter my feelings through the truth of Your Word.

This is the day that the Lord has made......I will rejoice and be glad in it!

My Daily Bread

Date:_____

Everything He gives me to do..............He's already provided a way to be done!

Opportunity Given	Provision Provided
_____	_____
_____	_____
_____	_____
_____	_____

Your will be done. Praises & Prayers

Answered

_____	_____
_____	_____
_____	_____
_____	_____

Forgive me as I forgive others.

_____
_____
_____

Character building moments in my refining process.

_____
_____
_____

Filter my feelings through the truth of Your Word.

_____
_____

This is the day that the Lord has made......I will rejoice and be glad in it!

My Daily Bread

Date:_____

Everything He gives me to do..............He's already provided a way to be done!

Opportunity Given	Provision Provided
_____	_____
_____	_____
_____	_____
_____	_____

Your will be done. Praises & Prayers

Answered

_____

_____

_____

_____

Forgive me as I forgive others.

Character building moments in my refining process.

Filter my feelings through the truth of Your Word.

This is the day that the Lord has made......I will rejoice and be glad in it!

My Daily Bread

Date:_____

Everything He gives me to do..............He's already provided a way to be done!

Opportunity Given	Provision Provided

Your will be done. Praises & Prayers

Answered

Forgive me as I forgive others.

Character building moments in my refining process.

Filter my feelings through the truth of Your Word.

This is the day that the Lord has made......I will rejoice and be glad in it!

My Daily Bread

Date:_____

Everything He gives me to do...............He's already provided a way to be done!

Opportunity Given	Provision Provided
_____	_____
_____	_____
_____	_____
_____	_____

Your will be done. Praises & Prayers

Answered

_____ _____
_____ _____
_____ _____
_____ _____

Forgive me as I forgive others.

_____
_____
_____

Character building moments in my refining process.

_____
_____

Filter my feelings through the truth of Your Word.

_____
_____

This is the day that the Lord has made......I will rejoice and be glad in it!

My Daily Bread

Date:_____

Everything He gives me to do..............He's already provided a way to be done!

Opportunity Given	Provision Provided
_____	_____
_____	_____
_____	_____
_____	_____

Your will be done. Praises & Prayers

Answered

_____ _____
_____ _____
_____ _____
_____ _____

Forgive me as I forgive others.

_____
_____
_____

Character building moments in my refining process.

_____
_____
_____

Filter my feelings through the truth of Your Word.

_____
_____

This is the day that the Lord has made......I will rejoice and be glad in it!

My Daily Bread

Date:_____

Everything He gives me to do..............He's already provided a way to be done!

Opportunity Given	Provision Provided
_____	_____
_____	_____
_____	_____
_____	_____

Your will be done. Praises & Prayers

Answered

_____ _____

_____ _____

_____ _____

_____ _____

Forgive me as I forgive others.

_____
_____
_____

Character building moments in my refining process.

_____
_____

Filter my feelings through the truth of Your Word.

_____
_____

This is the day that the Lord has made......I will rejoice and be glad in it!

My Daily Bread

Date:_____

Everything He gives me to do..............He's already provided a way to be done!

Opportunity Given	Provision Provided
_____	_____
_____	_____
_____	_____
_____	_____

Your will be done. Praises & Prayers

Answered

_____ _____

_____ _____

_____ _____

_____ _____

Forgive me as I forgive others.

_____

_____

_____

Character building moments in my refining process.

_____

_____

_____

Filter my feelings through the truth of Your Word.

_____

_____

This is the day that the Lord has made......I will rejoice and be glad in it!

My Daily Bread

Everything He gives me to do..............He's already provided a way to be done!

Opportunity Given	Provision Provided
_____	_____
_____	_____
_____	_____
_____	_____

Your will be done. Praises & Prayers

Answered

Forgive me as I forgive others.

Character building moments in my refining process.

Filter my feelings through the truth of Your Word.

This is the day that the Lord has made......I will rejoice and be glad in it!

My Daily Bread

Date:_____

Everything He gives me to do..............He's already provided a way to be done!

Opportunity Given	Provision Provided

Your will be done. Praises & Prayers

Answered

Forgive me as I forgive others.

Character building moments in my refining process.

Filter my feelings through the truth of Your Word.

This is the day that the Lord has made......I will rejoice and be glad in it!

My Daily Bread

Date:_____

Everything He gives me to do..............He's already provided a way to be done!

Opportunity Given	Provision Provided
_____	_____
_____	_____
_____	_____
_____	_____

Your will be done. Praises & Prayers

Answered

_____	_____
_____	_____
_____	_____
_____	_____

Forgive me as I forgive others.

_____
_____
_____

Character building moments in my refining process.

_____
_____

Filter my feelings through the truth of Your Word.

_____
_____

This is the day that the Lord has made......I will rejoice and be glad in it!

My Daily Bread

Date:_____

Everything He gives me to do...............He's already provided a way to be done!

Opportunity Given	Provision Provided

Your will be done. Praises & Prayers

Answered

Forgive me as I forgive others.

Character building moments in my refining process.

Filter my feelings through the truth of Your Word.

This is the day that the Lord has made......I will rejoice and be glad in it!

My Daily Bread

Date:_____

Everything He gives me to do..............He's already provided a way to be done!

Opportunity Given	Provision Provided
_____	_____
_____	_____
_____	_____
_____	_____

Your will be done. Praises & Prayers

Answered

_____ _____

_____ _____

_____ _____

_____ _____

Forgive me as I forgive others.

_____

_____

_____

Character building moments in my refining process.

_____

_____

_____

Filter my feelings through the truth of Your Word.

_____

_____

This is the day that the Lord has made......I will rejoice and be glad in it!

My Daily Bread

Date:_____

Everything He gives me to do..............He's already provided a way to be done!

Opportunity Given	Provision Provided
_____	_____
_____	_____
_____	_____
_____	_____

Your will be done. Praises & Prayers

Answered

_____ _____
_____ _____
_____ _____
_____ _____

Forgive me as I forgive others.

Character building moments in my refining process.

Filter my feelings through the truth of Your Word.

This is the day that the Lord has made......I will rejoice and be glad in it!

My Daily Bread

Date:_____

Everything He gives me to do..............He's already provided a way to be done!

Opportunity Given	Provision Provided
_____	_____
_____	_____
_____	_____
_____	_____

Your will be done. Praises & Prayers

Answered

Forgive me as I forgive others.

Character building moments in my refining process.

Filter my feelings through the truth of Your Word.

This is the day that the Lord has made......I will rejoice and be glad in it!

My Daily Bread

Date:_____

Everything He gives me to do..............He's already provided a way to be done!

Opportunity Given	Provision Provided
_____	_____
_____	_____
_____	_____
_____	_____

Your will be done. Praises & Prayers

Answered

_____ _____

_____ _____

_____ _____

_____ _____

Forgive me as I forgive others.

_____

_____

_____

Character building moments in my refining process.

_____

_____

_____

Filter my feelings through the truth of Your Word.

_____

_____

This is the day that the Lord has made......I will rejoice and be glad in it!

My Daily Bread

Date:_____

Everything He gives me to do...............He's already provided a way to be done!

Opportunity Given	Provision Provided
_____	_____
_____	_____
_____	_____
_____	_____

Your will be done. Praises & Prayers

Answered

_____ _____

_____ _____

_____ _____

_____ _____

Forgive me as I forgive others.

Character building moments in my refining process.

Filter my feelings through the truth of Your Word.

This is the day that the Lord has made......I will rejoice and be glad in it!

My Daily Bread

Date:_____

Everything He gives me to do..............He's already provided a way to be done!

Opportunity Given	Provision Provided
_____	_____
_____	_____
_____	_____
_____	_____

Your will be done. Praises & Prayers

Answered

_____	_____
_____	_____
_____	_____
_____	_____

Forgive me as I forgive others.

Character building moments in my refining process.

Filter my feelings through the truth of Your Word.

This is the day that the Lord has made......I will rejoice and be glad in it!

My Daily Bread

Date:_____

Everything He gives me to do..............He's already provided a way to be done!

Opportunity Given	Provision Provided
_____	_____
_____	_____
_____	_____
_____	_____

Your will be done. Praises & Prayers

Answered

_____ _____
_____ _____
_____ _____
_____ _____

Forgive me as I forgive others.

_____
_____
_____

Character building moments in my refining process.

_____
_____
_____

Filter my feelings through the truth of Your Word.

_____
_____

This is the day that the Lord has made......I will rejoice and be glad in it!

My Daily Bread

Date:_____

Everything He gives me to do..............He's already provided a way to be done!

Opportunity Given	Provision Provided
_____	_____
_____	_____
_____	_____
_____	_____

Your will be done. Praises & Prayers

Answered

Forgive me as I forgive others.

Character building moments in my refining process.

Filter my feelings through the truth of Your Word.

This is the day that the Lord has made......I will rejoice and be glad in it!

My Daily Bread

Date:_____

Everything He gives me to do...............He's already provided a way to be done!

Opportunity Given	Provision Provided
_____	_____
_____	_____
_____	_____
_____	_____

Your will be done. Praises & Prayers

Answered

_____ _____

_____ _____

_____ _____

_____ _____

Forgive me as I forgive others.

Character building moments in my refining process.

Filter my feelings through the truth of Your Word.

This is the day that the Lord has made......I will rejoice and be glad in it!

My Daily Bread

Date:_____

Everything He gives me to do...............He's already provided a way to be done!

Opportunity Given   Provision Provided

_____   _____

_____   _____

_____   _____

_____   _____

Your will be done. Praises & Prayers

Answered

_____   _____

_____   _____

_____   _____

_____   _____

Forgive me as I forgive others.

_____

_____

_____

Character building moments in my refining process.

_____

_____

_____

Filter my feelings through the truth of Your Word.

_____

_____

This is the day that the Lord has made......I will rejoice and be glad in it!

My Daily Bread

Date:_____

Everything He gives me to do..............He's already provided a way to be done!

Opportunity Given	Provision Provided
_____	_____
_____	_____
_____	_____
_____	_____

Your will be done. Praises & Prayers

Answered

_____	_____
_____	_____
_____	_____
_____	_____

Forgive me as I forgive others.

_____
_____
_____

Character building moments in my refining process.

_____
_____
_____

Filter my feelings through the truth of Your Word.

_____
_____

This is the day that the Lord has made......I will rejoice and be glad in it!

My Daily Bread

Date:_____

Everything He gives me to do..............He's already provided a way to be done!

Opportunity Given	Provision Provided
_____	_____
_____	_____
_____	_____
_____	_____

Your will be done. Praises & Prayers

Answered

_____ _____

_____ _____

_____ _____

_____ _____

Forgive me as I forgive others.

_____

_____

_____

Character building moments in my refining process.

_____

_____

_____

Filter my feelings through the truth of Your Word.

_____

_____

This is the day that the Lord has made......I will rejoice and be glad in it!

My Daily Bread

Date:_____

Everything He gives me to do..............He's already provided a way to be done!

Opportunity Given	Provision Provided
_____	_____
_____	_____
_____	_____
_____	_____

Your will be done. Praises & Prayers

Answered

_____ _____

_____ _____

_____ _____

_____ _____

Forgive me as I forgive others.

Character building moments in my refining process.

Filter my feelings through the truth of Your Word.

This is the day that the Lord has made......I will rejoice and be glad in it!

My Daily Bread

Date:_____

Everything He gives me to do..............He's already provided a way to be done!

Opportunity Given	Provision Provided
_____	_____
_____	_____
_____	_____
_____	_____

Your will be done. Praises & Prayers

Answered

_____	_____
_____	_____
_____	_____
_____	_____

Forgive me as I forgive others.

_____
_____
_____

Character building moments in my refining process.

_____
_____
_____

Filter my feelings through the truth of Your Word.

_____
_____

This is the day that the Lord has made......I will rejoice and be glad in it!

My Daily Bread

Date:_____

Everything He gives me to do..............He's already provided a way to be done!

Opportunity Given	Provision Provided

Your will be done. Praises & Prayers

Answered

Forgive me as I forgive others.

Character building moments in my refining process.

Filter my feelings through the truth of Your Word.

This is the day that the Lord has made......I will rejoice and be glad in it!

Notes

GENTLENESS

THE GODLY CHARACTER
OF GENTLENESS

"Let your gentleness be evident to all. The Lord is near" -Philippians 4:5

One of the characteristics of a true believer is their gentle spirit which can be described as a strong hand with a soft touch. They have a tender, compassionate approach toward others' weaknesses and limitations while speaking truth, sometimes even painful truth, but in a way that others can receive it.

Gentleness shouldn't be confused with weakness, nor does it come naturally. It is a learned trait that demonstrates the proper temperament or attitude for a servant of God that is in tune with the Holy Spirit.

Jesus displayed gentleness when He met the woman caught in adultery. The village leaders were yelling for her to be stoned and justice served. There was no compassion in their self-righteous hearts. But Jesus calmly wrote in the sand and said, "Let any one of you who is without sin be the first to throw a stone at her." One by one they dropped their stones and left. Then Jesus spoke truth to her, "Go now and leave your life of sin."

Jesus' words to the woman and His avoidance of violence and self-righteousness are examples of how God wants us to be with others. He wants us to demonstrate the power of His love with a gentle word of truth to a hurting world. He wants us to offer the same grace that we've received and He wants us to stop throwing stones.

We develop the godly character of gentleness when we start thinking about others more than ourselves. When we live with less judgement and more compassion and when we follow the example of Christ by speaking truth in love.

Jesus showed us the way and His example is a lamp to our feet and a light to our path. Remember, He never gives us gifts that we can't use.

BREAD FOR YOUR JOURNEY
GOD'S WORD CONCERNING GENTLENESS

Therefore, as God's chosen people, holy and dearly loved, clothe your-
selves with compassion, kindness, humility, gentleness and patience.

Colossians 3:12

A gentle answer turns away wrath,
but a harsh word stirs up anger.

Proverbs 15:1

Keep on loving one another as brothers and sisters. Do not for-
get to show hospitality to strangers, for by so doing some peo-
ple have shown hospitality to angels without knowing it.

Hebrews 13:1-2

But as for you, O man of God, flee these things. Pursue righteousness, godli-
ness, faith, love, steadfastness, gentleness. Fight the good fight of the faith.

1 Timothy 6:11-12

Gentle words are a tree of life; a deceitful tongue crushes the spirit.

Proverbs 15:4

Be wise in the way you act toward outsiders; make the most of every
opportunity. Let your conversation be always full of grace, sea-
soned with salt, so that you may know how to answer everyone.

Colossians 4:5-6

But in your hearts set apart Christ as Lord. Always be prepared to
give an answer to everyone who asks you to give the reason for the
hope that you have. But do this with gentleness and respect.

1 Peter 3:15

Checkpoints Along The Way

Expectations: What would change in my life if I had more Gentleness?

_____

_____

_____

_____

_____

Memorable Moments: What happened when I put Gentleness into practice?

_____

_____

_____

_____

_____

Reaping A Harvest: How has my life improved because of Gentleness?

_____

_____

_____

_____

_____

My Daily Bread

Date:_____

Everything He gives me to do..............He's already provided a way to be done!

Opportunity Given	Provision Provided
_____	_____
_____	_____
_____	_____
_____	_____

Your will be done. Praises & Prayers

Answered

_____ _____

_____ _____

_____ _____

_____ _____

Forgive me as I forgive others.

Character building moments in my refining process.

Filter my feelings through the truth of Your Word.

This is the day that the Lord has made......I will rejoice and be glad in it!

My Daily Bread

Date:_____

Everything He gives me to do..............He's already provided a way to be done!

Opportunity Given   Provision Provided

_____   _____

_____   _____

_____   _____

_____   _____

Your will be done. Praises & Prayers

Answered

_____   _____

_____   _____

_____   _____

_____   _____

Forgive me as I forgive others.

_____

_____

_____

Character building moments in my refining process.

_____

_____

_____

Filter my feelings through the truth of Your Word.

_____

_____

This is the day that the Lord has made......I will rejoice and be glad in it!

My Daily Bread

Date:_____

Everything He gives me to do..............He's already provided a way to be done!

Opportunity Given	Provision Provided
_____	_____
_____	_____
_____	_____
_____	_____

Your will be done. Praises & Prayers

Answered

_____	_____
_____	_____
_____	_____
_____	_____

Forgive me as I forgive others.

_____
_____
_____

Character building moments in my refining process.

_____
_____
_____

Filter my feelings through the truth of Your Word.

_____
_____

This is the day that the Lord has made......I will rejoice and be glad in it!

My Daily Bread

Date:_____

Everything He gives me to do..............He's already provided a way to be done!

Opportunity Given	Provision Provided
_____	_____
_____	_____
_____	_____
_____	_____

Your will be done. Praises & Prayers

Answered

_____ _____

_____ _____

_____ _____

_____ _____

Forgive me as I forgive others.

_____

_____

_____

Character building moments in my refining process.

_____

_____

_____

Filter my feelings through the truth of Your Word.

_____

_____

This is the day that the Lord has made......I will rejoice and be glad in it!

My Daily Bread

Date:_____

Everything He gives me to do..............He's already provided a way to be done!

Opportunity Given	Provision Provided
_____	_____
_____	_____
_____	_____
_____	_____

Your will be done. Praises & Prayers

Answered

_____ _____

_____ _____

_____ _____

_____ _____

Forgive me as I forgive others.

_____
_____
_____

Character building moments in my refining process.

_____
_____
_____

Filter my feelings through the truth of Your Word.

_____
_____

This is the day that the Lord has made......I will rejoice and be glad in it!

My Daily Bread

Date:_____

Everything He gives me to do..............He's already provided a way to be done!

Opportunity Given	Provision Provided
_____	_____
_____	_____
_____	_____
_____	_____

Your will be done. Praises & Prayers

Answered

_____ _____
_____ _____
_____ _____
_____ _____

Forgive me as I forgive others.

_____
_____
_____
_____

Character building moments in my refining process.

_____
_____
_____

Filter my feelings through the truth of Your Word.

_____
_____

This is the day that the Lord has made......I will rejoice and be glad in it!

My Daily Bread

Date:_____

Everything He gives me to do..............He's already provided a way to be done!

Opportunity Given   Provision Provided

_____   _____

_____   _____

_____   _____

_____   _____

Your will be done. Praises & Prayers

Answered

_____   _____

_____   _____

_____   _____

_____   _____

Forgive me as I forgive others.

_____

_____

_____

Character building moments in my refining process.

_____

_____

_____

Filter my feelings through the truth of Your Word.

_____

_____

This is the day that the Lord has made......I will rejoice and be glad in it!

My Daily Bread

Date:_____

Everything He gives me to do..............He's already provided a way to be done!

Opportunity Given	Provision Provided
_____	_____
_____	_____
_____	_____
_____	_____

Your will be done. Praises & Prayers

Answered

_____	_____
_____	_____
_____	_____
_____	_____

Forgive me as I forgive others.

_____
_____
_____

Character building moments in my refining process.

_____
_____
_____

Filter my feelings through the truth of Your Word.

_____
_____

This is the day that the Lord has made......I will rejoice and be glad in it!

My Daily Bread

Date:_____

Everything He gives me to do..............He's already provided a way to be done!

Opportunity Given	Provision Provided
_____	_____
_____	_____
_____	_____
_____	_____

Your will be done. Praises & Prayers

Answered

_____ _____

_____ _____

_____ _____

_____ _____

Forgive me as I forgive others.

Character building moments in my refining process.

Filter my feelings through the truth of Your Word.

This is the day that the Lord has made......I will rejoice and be glad in it!

My Daily Bread

Date:_____

Everything He gives me to do...............He's already provided a way to be done!

Opportunity Given	Provision Provided
_____	_____
_____	_____
_____	_____
_____	_____

Your will be done. Praises & Prayers

Answered

Forgive me as I forgive others.

Character building moments in my refining process.

Filter my feelings through the truth of Your Word.

This is the day that the Lord has made......I will rejoice and be glad in it!

My Daily Bread

Date:_____

Everything He gives me to do..............He's already provided a way to be done!

Opportunity Given	Provision Provided
_____	_____
_____	_____
_____	_____
_____	_____

Your will be done. Praises & Prayers .

Answered

_____ _____

_____ _____

_____ _____

_____ _____

Forgive me as I forgive others.

_____
_____
_____
_____

Character building moments in my refining process.

_____
_____
_____

Filter my feelings through the truth of Your Word.

_____
_____

This is the day that the Lord has made......I will rejoice and be glad in it!

My Daily Bread

Date:_____

Everything He gives me to do..............He's already provided a way to be done!

Opportunity Given	Provision Provided
_____	_____
_____	_____
_____	_____
_____	_____

Your will be done. Praises & Prayers

Answered

_____	_____
_____	_____
_____	_____
_____	_____

Forgive me as I forgive others.

Character building moments in my refining process.

Filter my feelings through the truth of Your Word.

This is the day that the Lord has made......I will rejoice and be glad in it!

My Daily Bread

Date:_____

Everything He gives me to do..............He's already provided a way to be done!

Opportunity Given	Provision Provided

Your will be done. Praises & Prayers

Answered

Forgive me as I forgive others.

Character building moments in my refining process.

Filter my feelings through the truth of Your Word.

This is the day that the Lord has made......I will rejoice and be glad in it!

My Daily Bread

Date:_____

Everything He gives me to do..............He's already provided a way to be done!

Opportunity Given	Provision Provided

Your will be done. Praises & Prayers

Answered

Forgive me as I forgive others.

Character building moments in my refining process.

Filter my feelings through the truth of Your Word.

This is the day that the Lord has made......I will rejoice and be glad in it!

My Daily Bread

Date:_____

Everything He gives me to do..............He's already provided a way to be done!

Opportunity Given	Provision Provided

Your will be done. Praises & Prayers

Answered

Forgive me as I forgive others.

Character building moments in my refining process.

Filter my feelings through the truth of Your Word.

This is the day that the Lord has made......I will rejoice and be glad in it!

My Daily Bread

Date:_____

Everything He gives me to do..............He's already provided a way to be done!

Opportunity Given	Provision Provided
_____	_____
_____	_____
_____	_____
_____	_____

Your will be done. Praises & Prayers

Answered

_____ _____

_____ _____

_____ _____

_____ _____

Forgive me as I forgive others.

_____

_____

_____

Character building moments in my refining process.

_____

_____

_____

Filter my feelings through the truth of Your Word.

_____

_____

This is the day that the Lord has made......I will rejoice and be glad in it!

My Daily Bread

Date:_____

Everything He gives me to do..............He's already provided a way to be done!

Opportunity Given	Provision Provided
_____	_____
_____	_____
_____	_____
_____	_____

Your will be done. Praises & Prayers

Answered

____ _____
____ _____
____ _____
____ _____

Forgive me as I forgive others.

_____
_____
_____
_____

Character building moments in my refining process.

_____
_____
_____

Filter my feelings through the truth of Your Word.

_____
_____

This is the day that the Lord has made......I will rejoice and be glad in it!

My Daily Bread

Date:_____

Everything He gives me to do...............He's already provided a way to be done!

Opportunity Given	Provision Provided

Your will be done. Praises & Prayers

Answered

Forgive me as I forgive others.

Character building moments in my refining process.

Filter my feelings through the truth of Your Word.

This is the day that the Lord has made......I will rejoice and be glad in it!

My Daily Bread

Date:_____

Everything He gives me to do..............He's already provided a way to be done!

Opportunity Given	Provision Provided
_____	_____
_____	_____
_____	_____
_____	_____

Your will be done. Praises & Prayers

Answered

Forgive me as I forgive others.

Character building moments in my refining process.

Filter my feelings through the truth of Your Word.

This is the day that the Lord has made......I will rejoice and be glad in it!

My Daily Bread

Date:_____

Everything He gives me to do..............He's already provided a way to be done!

Opportunity Given	Provision Provided
_____	_____
_____	_____
_____	_____
_____	_____

Your will be done. Praises & Prayers

Answered

_____ _____
_____ _____
_____ _____
_____ _____

Forgive me as I forgive others.

_____
_____
_____

Character building moments in my refining process.

_____
_____
_____

Filter my feelings through the truth of Your Word.

_____
_____

This is the day that the Lord has made......I will rejoice and be glad in it!

My Daily Bread

Date:_____

Everything He gives me to do..............He's already provided a way to be done!

Opportunity Given	Provision Provided
_____	_____
_____	_____
_____	_____
_____	_____

Your will be done. Praises & Prayers

Answered

_____ _____

_____ _____

_____ _____

_____ _____

Forgive me as I forgive others.

_____

_____

_____

Character building moments in my refining process.

_____

_____

_____

Filter my feelings through the truth of Your Word.

_____

_____

This is the day that the Lord has made......I will rejoice and be glad in it!

My Daily Bread

Date:_____

Everything He gives me to do..............He's already provided a way to be done!

Opportunity Given   Provision Provided

Your will be done. Praises & Prayers

Answered

Forgive me as I forgive others.

Character building moments in my refining process.

Filter my feelings through the truth of Your Word.

This is the day that the Lord has made......I will rejoice and be glad in it!

My Daily Bread

Date:_____

Everything He gives me to do..............He's already provided a way to be done!

Opportunity Given	Provision Provided
_____	_____
_____	_____
_____	_____
_____	_____

Your will be done. Praises & Prayers

Answered

_____
_____
_____
_____

Forgive me as I forgive others.

Character building moments in my refining process.

Filter my feelings through the truth of Your Word.

This is the day that the Lord has made......I will rejoice and be glad in it!

My Daily Bread

Date:_____

Everything He gives me to do..............He's already provided a way to be done!

Opportunity Given

Provision Provided

_____   _____

_____   _____

_____   _____

_____   _____

Your will be done. Praises & Prayers

Answered

_____

_____

_____

_____

Forgive me as I forgive others.

_____

_____

_____

_____

Character building moments in my refining process.

_____

_____

_____

_____

Filter my feelings through the truth of Your Word.

_____

_____

This is the day that the Lord has made......I will rejoice and be glad in it!

My Daily Bread

Date:_____

Everything He gives me to do..............He's already provided a way to be done!

Opportunity Given	Provision Provided
_____	_____
_____	_____
_____	_____
_____	_____

Your will be done. Praises & Prayers

Answered

_____ _____

_____ _____

_____ _____

_____ _____

Forgive me as I forgive others.

_____

_____

_____

_____

Character building moments in my refining process.

_____

_____

_____

Filter my feelings through the truth of Your Word.

_____

_____

This is the day that the Lord has made......I will rejoice and be glad in it!

My Daily Bread

Date:_____

Everything He gives me to do..............He's already provided a way to be done!

Opportunity Given   Provision Provided

Your will be done. Praises & Prayers

Answered

Forgive me as I forgive others.

Character building moments in my refining process.

Filter my feelings through the truth of Your Word.

This is the day that the Lord has made......I will rejoice and be glad in it!

My Daily Bread

Date:_____

Everything He gives me to do..............He's already provided a way to be done!

Opportunity Given	Provision Provided
_____	_____
_____	_____
_____	_____
_____	_____

Your will be done. Praises & Prayers

Answered

_____ _____

_____ _____

_____ _____

_____ _____

Forgive me as I forgive others.

_____

_____

_____

_____

Character building moments in my refining process.

_____

_____

_____

Filter my feelings through the truth of Your Word.

_____

_____

This is the day that the Lord has made......I will rejoice and be glad in it!

My Daily Bread

Date:_____

Everything He gives me to do..............He's already provided a way to be done!

Opportunity Given	Provision Provided
_____	_____
_____	_____
_____	_____
_____	_____

Your will be done. Praises & Prayers

Answered

_____ _____

_____ _____

_____ _____

_____ _____

Forgive me as I forgive others.

_____

_____

_____

Character building moments in my refining process.

_____

_____

_____

Filter my feelings through the truth of Your Word.

_____

_____

This is the day that the Lord has made......I will rejoice and be glad in it!

My Daily Bread

Date:_____

Everything He gives me to do..............He's already provided a way to be done!

Opportunity Given	Provision Provided
_____	_____
_____	_____
_____	_____
_____	_____

Your will be done. Praises & Prayers

Answered

_____   _____

_____   _____

_____   _____

_____   _____

Forgive me as I forgive others.

_____
_____
_____

Character building moments in my refining process.

_____
_____
_____

Filter my feelings through the truth of Your Word.

_____
_____

This is the day that the Lord has made......I will rejoice and be glad in it!

My Daily Bread

Date:_____

Everything He gives me to do..............He's already provided a way to be done!

Opportunity Given	Provision Provided
_____	_____
_____	_____
_____	_____
_____	_____

Your will be done. Praises & Prayers

Answered

_____ _____
_____ _____
_____ _____
_____ _____

Forgive me as I forgive others.

_____
_____
_____

Character building moments in my refining process.

_____
_____
_____

Filter my feelings through the truth of Your Word.

_____
_____

This is the day that the Lord has made......I will rejoice and be glad in it!

My Daily Bread

Date:_____

Everything He gives me to do..............He's already provided a way to be done!

Opportunity Given	Provision Provided
_____	_____
_____	_____
_____	_____
_____	_____

Your will be done. Praises & Prayers

Answered

_____	_____
_____	_____
_____	_____
_____	_____

Forgive me as I forgive others.

_____
_____
_____

Character building moments in my refining process.

_____
_____

Filter my feelings through the truth of Your Word.

_____
_____

This is the day that the Lord has made......I will rejoice and be glad in it!

Notes

SELF-CONTROL

THE GODLY CHARACTER
OF SELF -CONTROL

For God has not given us a spirit of fear and timidity, but
of power, love, and self-control. -2 Timothy 1:7

Self-control is a gift of the Holy Spirit. It has been defined as the ability to control your emotions and behavior in the face of temptations and impulses, but in our own efforts, we have all experienced a lack of self-control at one time or another.

It's only through the power of the Holy Spirit that we are able to resist the temptations that are common to man because He will not allow us to be tempted beyond what we are able to bear and He will provide a way of escape if we choose to follow His leading.

Jesus told us that in this world we will have trouble, but to take heart because He has overcome the world. He then gave His Holy Spirit to dwell within us and to be an advocate to help and be with us forever.

Exercising self-control might be hard, but we are strong enough in Christ. Jesus has won the battle, removed sin's power, and has empowered us to make the right choices. And because of that, we can say with confidence, "I can do all things through Christ who strengthens me."

When we feel like we're struggling with self-control, praying God's word becomes our life preserver. Jesus set the example when He was tempted by saying, "It is written…" and then repeatedly quoted scripture. God's word and prayer are effective weapons that will strengthen us and help us develop the godly character of self-control.

BREAD FOR YOUR JOURNEY
GOD'S WORD CONCERNING SELF-CONTROL

"He who is slow to anger is better than the mighty, and he
who rules his spirit, than he who captures a city."

Proverbs 16:32

My dear brothers and sisters, take note of this: Everyone should
be quick to listen, slow to speak and slow to become angry.

James 1:19

A fool is quick-tempered,

but a wise person stays calm when insulted.

Proverbs 12:16

For the grace of God has appeared that offers salvation to all people. It teaches
us to say "No" to ungodliness and worldly passions, and to live self-controlled,
upright and godly lives in this present age, while we wait for the blessed
hope—the appearing of the glory of our great God and Savior, Jesus Christ.

Titus 2: 10-13

Like a city whose walls are broken through is a person who lacks self-control.

Proverbs 25:28

Be self-controlled and alert. Your enemy the devil prowls around
like a roaring lion looking for someone to devour. Resist him, stand-
ing firm in the faith, because you know that your brothers throughout
the world are undergoing the same kind of sufferings. And the God of
all grace, who called you to his eternal glory in Christ, after you have
suffered a little while, will himself restore you and make you strong,
firm and steadfast. To him be the power forever and ever. Amen.

1 Peter 5:8-10

Checkpoints Along The Way

Expectations: What would change in my life if I had more Self Control?

_____

_____

_____

_____

_____

Memorable Moments: What happened when I put Self Control into practice?

_____

_____

_____

_____

Reaping A Harvest: How has my life improved because of Self Control?

_____

_____

_____

_____

_____

My Daily Bread

Date:_____

Everything He gives me to do..............He's already provided a way to be done!

Opportunity Given	Provision Provided
_____	_____
_____	_____
_____	_____
_____	_____

Your will be done. Praises & Prayers

Answered

_____ _____

_____ _____

_____ _____

_____ _____

Forgive me as I forgive others.

Character building moments in my refining process.

Filter my feelings through the truth of Your Word.

This is the day that the Lord has made......I will rejoice and be glad in it!

My Daily Bread

Date:_____

Everything He gives me to do..............He's already provided a way to be done!

Opportunity Given   Provision Provided

_____   _____

_____   _____

_____   _____

_____   _____

Your will be done. Praises & Prayers

Answered

_____   _____

_____   _____

_____   _____

_____   _____

Forgive me as I forgive others.

_____

_____

_____

Character building moments in my refining process.

_____

_____

_____

Filter my feelings through the truth of Your Word.

_____

_____

This is the day that the Lord has made......I will rejoice and be glad in it!

My Daily Bread   Date:_____

Everything He gives me to do..............He's already provided a way to be done!

Opportunity Given	Provision Provided

Your will be done. Praises & Prayers

Answered

Forgive me as I forgive others.

Character building moments in my refining process.

Filter my feelings through the truth of Your Word.

This is the day that the Lord has made......I will rejoice and be glad in it!

My Daily Bread

Everything He gives me to do..............He's already provided a way to be done!

Opportunity Given   Provision Provided

_____   _____

_____   _____

_____   _____

_____   _____

Your will be done. Praises & Prayers

Answered

_____   _____

_____   _____

_____   _____

_____   _____

Forgive me as I forgive others.

_____

_____

_____

Character building moments in my refining process.

_____

_____

_____

Filter my feelings through the truth of Your Word.

_____

_____

This is the day that the Lord has made......I will rejoice and be glad in it!

My Daily Bread

Date:_____

Everything He gives me to do..............He's already provided a way to be done!

Opportunity Given	Provision Provided

Your will be done. Praises & Prayers

Answered

Forgive me as I forgive others.

Character building moments in my refining process.

Filter my feelings through the truth of Your Word.

This is the day that the Lord has made......I will rejoice and be glad in it!

My Daily Bread

Date:_____

Everything He gives me to do..............He's already provided a way to be done!

Opportunity Given	Provision Provided
_____	_____
_____	_____
_____	_____
_____	_____

Your will be done. Praises & Prayers

Answered

_____ _____

_____ _____

_____ _____

_____ _____

Forgive me as I forgive others.

Character building moments in my refining process.

Filter my feelings through the truth of Your Word.

This is the day that the Lord has made.......I will rejoice and be glad in it!

My Daily Bread

Date:_____

Everything He gives me to do...............He's already provided a way to be done!

Opportunity Given	Provision Provided
_____	_____
_____	_____
_____	_____
_____	_____

Your will be done. Praises & Prayers

Answered

_____ _____

_____ _____

_____ _____

_____ _____

Forgive me as I forgive others.

_____

_____

_____

Character building moments in my refining process.

_____

_____

_____

Filter my feelings through the truth of Your Word.

_____

_____

This is the day that the Lord has made......I will rejoice and be glad in it!

My Daily Bread

Date:_____

Everything He gives me to do..............He's already provided a way to be done!

Opportunity Given	Provision Provided
_____	_____
_____	_____
_____	_____
_____	_____

Your will be done. Praises & Prayers

Answered

Forgive me as I forgive others.

Character building moments in my refining process.

Filter my feelings through the truth of Your Word.

This is the day that the Lord has made......I will rejoice and be glad in it!

My Daily Bread

Date:_____

Everything He gives me to do...............He's already provided a way to be done!

Opportunity Given	Provision Provided
_____	_____
_____	_____
_____	_____
_____	_____

Your will be done. Praises & Prayers

Answered

_____ _____

_____ _____

_____ _____

_____ _____

Forgive me as I forgive others.

_____

_____

_____

Character building moments in my refining process.

_____

_____

_____

Filter my feelings through the truth of Your Word.

_____

_____

This is the day that the Lord has made......I will rejoice and be glad in it!

My Daily Bread

Date:_____

Everything He gives me to do..............He's already provided a way to be done!

Opportunity Given	Provision Provided

Your will be done. Praises & Prayers

Answered

Forgive me as I forgive others.

Character building moments in my refining process.

Filter my feelings through the truth of Your Word.

This is the day that the Lord has made......I will rejoice and be glad in it!

My Daily Bread

Date:_____

Everything He gives me to do..............He's already provided a way to be done!

Opportunity Given	Provision Provided
_____	_____
_____	_____
_____	_____
_____	_____

Your will be done. Praises & Prayers

Answered

_____ _____

_____ _____

_____ _____

_____ _____

Forgive me as I forgive others.

_____

_____

_____

Character building moments in my refining process.

_____

_____

_____

Filter my feelings through the truth of Your Word.

_____

_____

This is the day that the Lord has made......I will rejoice and be glad in it!

My Daily Bread

Date:_____

Everything He gives me to do..............He's already provided a way to be done!

Opportunity Given   Provision Provided

_____   _____

_____   _____

_____   _____

_____   _____

Your will be done. Praises & Prayers

Answered

_____   _____

_____   _____

_____   _____

_____   _____

Forgive me as I forgive others.

_____

_____

_____

Character building moments in my refining process.

_____

_____

_____

Filter my feelings through the truth of Your Word.

_____

_____

This is the day that the Lord has made......I will rejoice and be glad in it!

My Daily Bread

Date:_____

Everything He gives me to do..............He's already provided a way to be done!

Opportunity Given	Provision Provided
_____	_____
_____	_____
_____	_____
_____	_____

Your will be done. Praises & Prayers

Answered

_____	_____
_____	_____
_____	_____
_____	_____

Forgive me as I forgive others.

_____

Character building moments in my refining process.

_____

Filter my feelings through the truth of Your Word.

_____

This is the day that the Lord has made......I will rejoice and be glad in it!

My Daily Bread

Date:_____

Everything He gives me to do..............He's already provided a way to be done!

Opportunity Given	Provision Provided
_____	_____
_____	_____
_____	_____
_____	_____

Your will be done. Praises & Prayers

Answered

_____ _____
_____ _____
_____ _____
_____ _____

Forgive me as I forgive others.

_____
_____
_____

Character building moments in my refining process.

_____
_____
_____

Filter my feelings through the truth of Your Word.

_____
_____

This is the day that the Lord has made......I will rejoice and be glad in it!

My Daily Bread

Date:_____

Everything He gives me to do..............He's already provided a way to be done!

Opportunity Given	Provision Provided
_____	_____
_____	_____
_____	_____
_____	_____

Your will be done. Praises & Prayers

Answered

_____ _____

_____ _____

_____ _____

_____ _____

Forgive me as I forgive others.

_____

_____

_____

Character building moments in my refining process.

_____

_____

_____

Filter my feelings through the truth of Your Word.

_____

_____

This is the day that the Lord has made......I will rejoice and be glad in it!

My Daily Bread

Date:_____

Everything He gives me to do..............He's already provided a way to be done!

Opportunity Given   Provision Provided

_____   _____

_____   _____

_____   _____

_____   _____

Your will be done. Praises & Prayers

Answered

_____   _____

_____   _____

_____   _____

_____   _____

Forgive me as I forgive others.

_____

_____

_____

Character building moments in my refining process.

_____

_____

_____

Filter my feelings through the truth of Your Word.

_____

_____

This is the day that the Lord has made.......I will rejoice and be glad in it!

My Daily Bread

Date:_____

Everything He gives me to do..............He's already provided a way to be done!

Opportunity Given	Provision Provided
_____	_____
_____	_____
_____	_____
_____	_____

Your will be done. Praises & Prayers

Answered

_____ _____

_____ _____

_____ _____

_____ _____

Forgive me as I forgive others.

_____

_____

_____

Character building moments in my refining process.

_____

_____

Filter my feelings through the truth of Your Word.

_____

_____

This is the day that the Lord has made......I will rejoice and be glad in it!

My Daily Bread

Date:_____

Everything He gives me to do..............He's already provided a way to be done!

Opportunity Given	Provision Provided
_____	_____
_____	_____
_____	_____
_____	_____

Your will be done. Praises & Prayers

Answered

Forgive me as I forgive others.

Character building moments in my refining process.

Filter my feelings through the truth of Your Word.

This is the day that the Lord has made......I will rejoice and be glad in it!

My Daily Bread

Date: _____

Everything He gives me to do..............He's already provided a way to be done!

Opportunity Given	Provision Provided
_____	_____
_____	_____
_____	_____
_____	_____

Your will be done. Praises & Prayers

Answered

_____ _____

_____ _____

_____ _____

_____ _____

Forgive me as I forgive others.

_____

_____

_____

Character building moments in my refining process.

_____

_____

_____

Filter my feelings through the truth of Your Word.

_____

_____

This is the day that the Lord has made......I will rejoice and be glad in it!

My Daily Bread

Date:_____

Everything He gives me to do..............He's already provided a way to be done!

Opportunity Given	Provision Provided
_____	_____
_____	_____
_____	_____
_____	_____

Your will be done. Praises & Prayers

Answered

_____ _____
_____ _____
_____ _____
_____ _____

Forgive me as I forgive others.

_____
_____
_____

Character building moments in my refining process.

_____
_____
_____

Filter my feelings through the truth of Your Word.

_____
_____

This is the day that the Lord has made......I will rejoice and be glad in it!

My Daily Bread

Date:_____

Everything He gives me to do..............He's already provided a way to be done!

Opportunity Given	Provision Provided
_____	_____
_____	_____
_____	_____
_____	_____

Your will be done. Praises & Prayers

Answered

_____ _____

_____ _____

_____ _____

_____ _____

Forgive me as I forgive others.

_____

_____

_____

Character building moments in my refining process.

_____

_____

Filter my feelings through the truth of Your Word.

_____

_____

This is the day that the Lord has made......I will rejoice and be glad in it!

My Daily Bread

Date:_____

Everything He gives me to do...............He's already provided a way to be done!

Opportunity Given	Provision Provided
_____	_____
_____	_____
_____	_____
_____	_____

Your will be done. Praises & Prayers

Answered

_____ _____

_____ _____

_____ _____

_____ _____

Forgive me as I forgive others.

Character building moments in my refining process.

Filter my feelings through the truth of Your Word.

This is the day that the Lord has made......I will rejoice and be glad in it!

My Daily Bread

Date:_____

Everything He gives me to do..............He's already provided a way to be done!

Opportunity Given	Provision Provided
_____	_____
_____	_____
_____	_____
_____	_____

Your will be done. Praises & Prayers

Answered

_____   _____

_____   _____

_____   _____

_____   _____

Forgive me as I forgive others.

Character building moments in my refining process.

Filter my feelings through the truth of Your Word.

This is the day that the Lord has made......I will rejoice and be glad in it!

My Daily Bread

Date:_____

Everything He gives me to do..............He's already provided a way to be done!

Opportunity Given	Provision Provided
_____	_____
_____	_____
_____	_____
_____	_____

Your will be done. Praises & Prayers

Answered

_____ _____

_____ _____

_____ _____

_____ _____

Forgive me as I forgive others.

_____

_____

_____

Character building moments in my refining process.

_____

_____

_____

Filter my feelings through the truth of Your Word.

_____

_____

This is the day that the Lord has made......I will rejoice and be glad in it!

My Daily Bread

Date:_____

Everything He gives me to do..............He's already provided a way to be done!

Opportunity Given	Provision Provided
_____	_____
_____	_____
_____	_____
_____	_____

Your will be done. Praises & Prayers

Answered

_____   _____

_____   _____

_____   _____

_____   _____

Forgive me as I forgive others.

_____

_____

_____

Character building moments in my refining process.

_____

_____

_____

Filter my feelings through the truth of Your Word.

_____

_____

This is the day that the Lord has made......I will rejoice and be glad in it!

My Daily Bread

Date:_____

Everything He gives me to do..............He's already provided a way to be done!

Opportunity Given	Provision Provided
_____	_____
_____	_____
_____	_____
_____	_____

Your will be done. Praises & Prayers

Answered

_____ _____

_____ _____

_____ _____

_____ _____

Forgive me as I forgive others.

_____

_____

_____

Character building moments in my refining process.

_____

_____

_____

Filter my feelings through the truth of Your Word.

_____

_____

This is the day that the Lord has made......I will rejoice and be glad in it!

My Daily Bread

Date:_____

Everything He gives me to do..............He's already provided a way to be done!

Opportunity Given	Provision Provided
_____	_____
_____	_____
_____	_____
_____	_____

Your will be done. Praises & Prayers

Answered

Forgive me as I forgive others.

Character building moments in my refining process.

Filter my feelings through the truth of Your Word.

This is the day that the Lord has made......I will rejoice and be glad in it!

My Daily Bread

Date:_____

Everything He gives me to do..............He's already provided a way to be done!

Opportunity Given	Provision Provided
_____	_____
_____	_____
_____	_____
_____	_____

Your will be done. Praises & Prayers

Answered

_____ _____
_____ _____
_____ _____
_____ _____

Forgive me as I forgive others.

_____
_____
_____

Character building moments in my refining process.

_____
_____
_____

Filter my feelings through the truth of Your Word.

_____
_____

This is the day that the Lord has made......I will rejoice and be glad in it!

My Daily Bread

Date:_____

Everything He gives me to do..............He's already provided a way to be done!

Opportunity Given	Provision Provided
_____	_____
_____	_____
_____	_____
_____	_____

Your will be done. Praises & Prayers

Answered

_____ _____

_____ _____

_____ _____

_____ _____

Forgive me as I forgive others.

_____

_____

_____

Character building moments in my refining process.

_____

_____

_____

Filter my feelings through the truth of Your Word.

_____

_____

This is the day that the Lord has made......I will rejoice and be glad in it!

My Daily Bread

Date:_____

Everything He gives me to do..............He's already provided a way to be done!

Opportunity Given	Provision Provided
_____	_____
_____	_____
_____	_____
_____	_____

Your will be done. Praises & Prayers

Answered

_____ _____

_____ _____

_____ _____

_____ _____

Forgive me as I forgive others.

_____

_____

_____

Character building moments in my refining process.

_____

_____

_____

Filter my feelings through the truth of Your Word.

_____

_____

This is the day that the Lord has made......I will rejoice and be glad in it!

My Daily Bread

Date:_____

Everything He gives me to do..............He's already provided a way to be done!

Opportunity Given	Provision Provided
_____	_____
_____	_____
_____	_____
_____	_____

Your will be done. Praises & Prayers

Answered

_____

_____

_____

_____

Forgive me as I forgive others.

Character building moments in my refining process.

Filter my feelings through the truth of Your Word.

This is the day that the Lord has made......I will rejoice and be glad in it!

Notes